DIRTY WORK

ANNA MAXYMIW

DIRTY WORK

My Gruelling, Glorious, Life-Changing
Summer in the Wilderness

McCLELLAND & STEWART

Library and Archives Canada Cataloguing in Publication

Maxymiw, Anna, author
Dirty work : my gruelling, glorious, life-changing summer
in the wilderness / Anna Maxymiw.

Issued in print and electronic formats.
ISBN 978-0-7710-6146-2 (softcover).—ISBN 978-0-7710-6147-9 (EPUB)

1. Maxymiw, Anna. 2. Fishing lodges—Ontario. 3. Outdoor life.
4. Self-actualization (Psychology). 5. Authors, Canadian (English)—
21st century—Biography. I. Title.

SH439.M39 2019   799.1   C2018-903254-5
                                       C2018-903255-3

Cover art: boat © Chris Clor/Tetra images/Getty Images
cleaning supplies © DragonImages/iStock/Getty Images
Cover design by Five Seventeen

Typeset in Harriet by M&S, Toronto
Printed and bound in Canada

McClelland & Stewart,
a division of Penguin Random House Canada Limited,
a Penguin Random House Company
www.penguinrandomhouse.ca

1 2 3 4 5   23 22 21 20 19

Penguin
Random House
McCLELLAND & STEWART

To the dockhands and the guides and the housekeepers

The forests are making magic against us—
I think the land knows we are here,
I think the land knows we are strangers.
—Al Purdy, "The Runners"

THE LAND OF LITTLE STICKS

"DHC-2 Beavers stopped being produced in 1967, you know," the pilot tells me with a shit-wild grin. I can't see his eyes behind his huge sunglasses, but I know that he's hungover from the way he speaks, and the way he slung himself into the front seat of the plane. By that logic, the de Havilland floatplane I'm sitting in is just about fifty years old, and it looks it—worn grey seats, ancient controls, a smeared windshield.

I clench at his words, regretting all the decisions I made that have led me to this point. Deciding to spend a summer in remote Northern Ontario was all well and good when I was in the city, but now that I'm here, at the very moment we're about to depart, I begin to panic. Nothing about this—the pilot, the plane, my surroundings—is reassuring.

Some people might call it brave, the act of getting away and stepping so far out of one's comfort zone. But I don't feel brave. Instead, I feel my thighs start to sweat, my skin sticking to the plane seat and the skin of the two girls who are wedged in on either side of me. On my left is Sydney, to my right is Robin, and in the front seat, there's Connor. I'm too wrapped up in a complicated web of nerves and regret and a strange form of excitement to feel brave. None of us speaks.

"If you need to puke," the pilot continues, filling our silence, "there are barf bags in the backs of the seats in front of you." When I reach into the pocket he's referring to, I pull out flimsy plastic shopping bags, which are full of holes.

Behind me, the plane reverberates with a dull *thunk* as a member of the air base staff throws my duffel bag into the boot and slams the door. My palms are damp and my mouth is dry; I try not to move my hands around too much, so the others won't notice that I'm shaking. *It's not too late*, I tell myself, *to get the hell out of here.* It's not too late to unbuckle my seatbelt and wriggle out from between this sweaty female flesh, climb over hips and stomachs, and fling myself out of the plane and back onto dry land. I could tear my bag out of the back if I really wanted to; I could kick up a fuss. I could leave and spend my summer in a different place, a place where I won't run into black bears, where I won't have to spend nine weeks cleaning up after middle-aged men, where I can step outside and blackflies won't immediately gather on my eyebrows and temples like a bloodthirsty crown. That would be the easy choice. Because I know that nothing about where I'm going will be easy. I know that because I've been there once before, and I'm scared to return in a different capacity, scared to revisit this place that has hung, wild and lush and gesturing, in my dreams for a year.

The propeller starts with a thunderous moan, and I jump. The sound fills the tiny plane body, all-consuming; it vibrates into my bones, all the way up to my teeth, like the purr of a huge, rusty cat finally getting attention; it crowds me so much that there isn't space for doubt. There's only space for momentum, for self-preservation, so I yank the padded headset over my ears, double-check that my seatbelt is buckled, and curl my fingers under the lip of the seat. *There's nowhere to go but forward. There's nothing to do but take off.*

Three other planes have gone up before us, carrying cargo and the rest of my co-workers. We four are the last to be delivered of thirteen young adults from different towns all around the province, mostly strangers to one another—all of us running on empty stomachs and a bad night's sleep at the air base's piece-of-shit bunkhouse—about to spend late May to late July working together at a fishing lodge in the Northern Ontario bush.

* * *

Northern Canada: "The land of little sticks." It's a part of the country that evokes divisive emotions in those who have seen it or live on it—or have tried to live on it—and now it's going to be my home for the summer. I've done a little bit of reading on this place. I wanted to know what people had to say about it, bad or good, whether they were entranced or repulsed. "The land that God gave to Cain," Jacques Cartier wrote when describing the northern forests of Quebec. I can't help but replay those words to myself as I think about the summer ahead. In fact, Northern Canada was deemed so worthless that, in 1670, England's King Charles II gave the land away—7.7 million square kilometres of it—to the Hudson's Bay Company, which, it might be said, turned a good profit off of it. And so Northern Canada, this tangle of bog, fen, black spruce, and myth, is known as many things, depending on who you speak to: the nothing; the North; a wasteland; a dream destination; a place of infinite and strange beauty.

Our destination, Kesagami Wilderness Lodge, is in the Hudson Bay Lowlands, a geological region defined by peat bog and wide, slow-moving rivers, which sits about a hundred kilometres south of James Bay, near the Quebec border. You can't drive to where we're going. The labyrinth of trees and water stops you in your tracks. Roads end as if you're about to drive off the Earth. So, we made our way by train through the Canadian Shield, that ancient plate of granite that grips half of our country, unforgiving rock that had to be blasted through to build roads and the railway. We're heading for the middle of Kesagami Provincial Park, to the eastern side of Kesagami Lake—a big body of water, about 32 kilometres long and 12 kilometres at its widest, with about 290 kilometres of shoreline. *Kesagami* means "big water" in Cree, and the name is fitting. Big water, big land, big fish, big possibility.

* * *

Our plane lurches alive. I grab my elbows and brace my body as the Beaver's prop revs up to full tilt and the plane fills with a roar that makes it impossible to yell, let alone talk—if we had been talking to one another in the first place. The plane jerks forward and then turns, near the end of the lake, readying for takeoff. I'd ask the pilot a million questions about safety, about how long he has to make his decision about when to lift the plane up into flight before he runs out of lake, but he wouldn't hear me. We accelerate, the pontoons carving out a wake and the end of the lake approaching in our windshield, faster and faster, and then we're hovering over the surface of the water, dragging out a spray, before the whole machine scuds gracelessly up, up, up, and we're in the air, and there's no turning back.

I look ahead. My ears pop and I sit as ramrod straight as I can, trying not to give in to curiosity, because I'm worried I'll get nauseated and have to use those hopeless barf bags in front of these strangers. As we get higher and higher, I turn my head to peep out the window over Robin's shoulder. I'm blown away all over again, even though I've seen this before. A few minutes into the flight and we're already approaching the boundary where the Canadian North really, truly begins. The boreal forest, also known as the taiga, is a biome—an ecological community. It's a huge terrestrial area, a swath of cold forest that slices across the top of the world map. Worldwide, the taiga measures about twelve million square kilometres, and Canada comprises 24 per cent of this. We'll be flying into an area where the taiga is at its narrowest, pinched tight around the tip of James Bay.

As the plane tilts, the windows are at a direct angle to the morning sun, which is prisming across the clean sky and scattering over the water below me, and then bouncing up into our plane. An overpowering light slants through the smeary plastic and lands on my palms. I look around in silent awe as the sun laces into the tips of my hair and across my body, creating a circuit, filling the plane and filling me. The four of us go from singular beings, damp and miserable in nervousness and nausea from the bouncing little plane, to a group forged in gold in the span of an instant that is saturated and alive and gleaming. Every surface is lit up, everything bright, almost painfully halcyon. I wonder if this is a sign of good things to come; the anxiety curled up like a tiny beast behind my breastbone starts to unwind, just a little.

There aren't words to describe the vastness of the land below us—the green depths of the forest that stretches farther than the horizon, the occasional ribbon of brown where a decrepit logging road braids through the woods. This is Northern Ontario, and the sight of it makes me feel like all of the air has been struck out of my lungs.

As we go farther north, the forest dimples and tatters, and the trees start to give way to swampy ground, a terrain that looks gnarled and odd to my eye, twisted up in shades of lime and amber. These are the lowlands, an area formed by the ebb and flow of ancient seas and the rise and fall of ancient mountains, a place apparently so uninhabitable that not all of it has been explored. Who knows what lives in the foliage below our pontoons? Or, for that matter, in the water. Dotted into the land are hundreds and hundreds of lakes—intricate, myriad, shimmering bodies of water of various sizes. As employees, our lives up here are going to revolve around water. Though we're going to live on the land, it's the lake that's the star attraction. It pulls people to it, has the power to give and take life, and contains the fish that draw people to the lodge from across the continent. But right now, so high up, I can't think about the fish, the depth, what lives below the surface. I can only stare at the shimmering skeins of lake unfolding before me, kilometre after kilometre after kilometre of watery divots dappling the green.

It's like tracing the footsteps of giants, travelling back in time. I'm glad that the prop rumble is so overpowering that I wouldn't be able to voice my thoughts if they managed to slither out of my mouth. But in the untapped part of me, there's a feeling that the forests below hold secrets that none of us would be able to whisper. That below these wings are monsters and gods: bears taller than me, pike as long as children, things that lurk in the latticework of the woods. That agreeing to work at this lodge this summer is the smartest or stupidest thing I've ever done.

As the plane nears our destination, Sydney presses her face to the window, and I follow suit, slotting my sticky torso against hers. If she minds, she doesn't say anything. Something about a fist-clenched plane ride and being in close quarters has set us at ease; our bodies are already comfortable around each other, even if our minds haven't caught up. The colours of the land swell into mottled, rich browns and taupes, rust reds, and vivid greens; the earth has plaited itself into the water, and in places where it looks like soil, I instinctively know there's water there, too, hiding and waiting. The lakes that looked like footsteps have given way to footstep greenery, the land no longer dominant.

A saucer of thick water expands in the windshield of the plane, broadening like a swath of brown velvet unwrapped. My heart thumps; I recognize this sight. I remember these curves and corners and white sand. The lake grows in front of us as we get closer and closer, and the sun hits its surface, the morning light dancing up in hues of black and silver and white and beige. And then we're tilting down, down, down, and I watch as we hover over the water for what seems like minutes, and then there's a great wake, a lurch and a hum, the propeller slowing its roar as the plane sputters up to the dock, my pulse taking over that rhythm. The smell of not-city forces its way past the windows and into the plane, curling its hands around our necks and stroking our lips with its fingers—it's the smell of diesel and algae and lake water and something else, something I can't put words to.

We fall out of the plane to lots of laughter. I can see figures on the shore, hear a chorus of male snickering. The interlock dock beneath me is too unsteady, and I'm unmoored, a stranger here.

In desperation, I squint and look at the silhouettes: the sun's so strong behind them that I can't see faces, only the outlines of ears and jaws and ball caps. As I stare, one of the figures cocks a head. We're being watched, right away, taken stock of and slotted into people's minds based on our bodies and our postures and the way we hold our duffel bags. This is my first chance to make an impression, and I'm frozen, looking back at the person who is looking at me, my damp hair coiling around my chin from the high whip of the northern wind, my heart limping in an unsure tattoo.

I can't move—won't move, won't cede to this standoff—and then Henry, the lodge manager, walks toward us, saluting us with chores already on his lips, and the moment is broken. When I look to the shore, the boys have scattered, and somehow, inelegantly, suddenly, the summer has begun.

WELCOME TO THE SUMMER, ASSHOLES

"You're going to have to run that by me again," says Jack, head fishing guide and veteran employee of five years. We're standing in the lodge's dining room after a whirlwind tour of the camp, led by Alex and Tiffany, our head housekeepers for the summer, and therefore the two girls who will direct the rest of us regular housekeepers. My brain is flooded with so much information I feel like my eyes are spinning. Now we're trying on staff shirts, and the veteran female employees have introduced the new girls to the boys.

"Because I'm not gonna fuckin' remember any of your names," Jack continues, chewing on his spit.

Really, he has the easier job when it comes to retaining information. The rest of us haven't even been here two hours, and already we've been given a hurried, haphazard history of the lodge and geography lessons about the land we're staying on. So far, I've learned that Kesagami lodge is an old beast, one that's changed hands a few times over its life. It was founded in 1983 by a Swiss couple when they bought out an outfitter. Over the span of nearly three years, and with the help of large sums of money and many, many supply flights, the site expanded from its original six cabins and became a semblance of what the lodge is today. In 1992, an American couple purchased the lodge, and they implemented the strict fishing policies that survive on the lake.

Now, I hear, ownership is transitioning to the Moose Cree First Nation band, a Cree First Nation from Moose Factory. Moose Factory is a community of about twenty-five hundred people located on Moose Factory Island, near the mouth of the Moose River, in the south of James Bay. It's the town that's technically the closest to us by helicopter or floatplane; it's where we'd be flown if we suffered an emergency at the lodge. People can take water taxis back and forth between Moose Factory and its sister town, Moosonee, or, in the winter, drive the ice road between them. It's comforting to know that there's an out if we need it; somewhat nearby, there are roads and a hospital and a population of more than twenty-five.

A few of the veterans spoke of the leadership change on the train ride up. I caught snatches of the conversation from in between upholstered seats. *What do you think it means? What will future summers look like? Does this mean the summer will be more difficult? Does this mean we'll be working harder? Not as hard? Will the new bosses be benevolent or cruel? Will they drop in for inspections? What, what, what.* The vets had no answers to these panicky questions, still don't, so we're all walking into the summer blind, it seems.

I don't really have any thoughts on the change of owners. It seems like the owners are never really at the lodge, anyway; it's

Henry who spends the whole summer at Kesagami, figuring out the day-to-day ins and outs, bossing the employees around, making the rules that we have to follow. I'm not worried; it seems unlikely that the owners will have much influence on us. I am, however, surprised at the complexity of the situation. We're living on Indigenous land, and it seems odd that Indigenous people have to purchase the lodge from white people. Did the original Swiss owners buy this land? If so, from whom did they buy it? Or did they set up the lodge in the same way that settlers have often stolen Indigenous land—just doing it, not asking, not apologizing? These are the questions orbiting my head as I try to get my bearings here once more.

Kesagami is how I remember it: set up in an odd sprawl, held together with hope and grit, and not quite making sense in the way it's organized. The central hub is one big building that contains the bar, the kitchen, the dining room. The dining room is where all the hustle and bustle is, where everyone gathers: there's a small tackle shop in one corner, rows of gleaming maple tables lit up by the stained-glass windows showing images of walleye and pike, fireplaces for guests to sit around, a pool table where I remember rowdy fishermen clustering to shoot the shit some nights. The room is decorated as a wilderness lodge is always decorated—taxidermied animals, including a tall stuffed black bear that looms in the corner opposite to the tackle counter, that give off the rich, ripe scent of old fur; a mottled carpet that releases dust motes into the air whenever you walk on it; old lures and hooks and pictures of trophy fish, guests from the past grinning with their big catches, all over the walls. It's a throwback, everything a bit out of date and the decor more than a little tacky. There's even an entire ancient moose pelt stretched out over the east wall. Still, as far as wilderness lodges go, it's luxurious in that it has running water, generator electricity, hot meals cooked by a chef.

At the back of the main building, beyond the gloss and glow of the dining room, the staff perform duties that are unseen by the guests. This part of the lodge, the kitchen, is new to me. To get to the kitchen, you have to go through the dining room to a pair of doors—one in, and one out—which both seem to swing too easily on their old hinges. Beyond the kitchen, there's the narrow and dark pantry, holding tubs of peanut butter and buckets of barbecue sauce and other condiments and dry goods. Beyond the pantry, there's a tiny staff dining room, complete with a chipped table, smudged windows, a sloping ceiling. Across from the staff dining room is a storage space that leads to Henry's bedroom, which also doubles as his office.

Exiting from the back door of the lodge leads to a three-pronged path. One direction takes you through a little thicket to the motel, the premium place to stay at Kesagami. The motel has ten rooms, each with its own baseboard heater and bathroom, but no real insulation, so every movement, fart, groan, and bone-pop can be heard. Take another path and you walk straight into the forest, past a wood yard. The final path leads to the guest cabins—eight of them, spread out through the trees, connected only by winding, barely visible dirt trails. Fishermen who want a more rustic experience—translated: people who don't want to pay through the nose for a motel room where you can hear your neighbour pass gas—book the cabins, which have electricity but no heat, so guests make their own fires in the stoves provided. They sleep in damp-sheeted bunk beds and fend off spiders that crawl through the cracks in the walls; if they have to go to the bathroom, they walk to the bathhouse, one building that has two flushing toilets for the men and one flushing toilet for women, a few urinals on the outside of the shack, and a couple of showers.

There are thirteen cabins in total: eight for guests, five for staff. The "old man shack" is where the older guides and Sam, the cook, stay, wedged into tiny, dark bunks. Cabin 6, which used to be a guest cabin, is where the new boys sleep. Right behind Cabin 6 is the pebbly staff beach—we're not allowed to swim at the waterfront, which is reserved solely for the guests. The returning male staff members sleep in the "guideshack," a new, nice-smelling building with big bunks and lots of windows. The returning female staff quickly snap up the "front girls cabin," a large, squat cube of a bunkhouse right on the waterfront. The cabin has a sign on it that says *Rigi Stube* in red block letters, a remnant of the original Swiss ownership. No one asks what it means; there are too many other things to figure out at the moment.

The new girls are sent to the "back girls cabin," the old bunkhouse behind the lodge, at the edge of the trees. The back cabin is a sight. It's shitty and old and its logs are chinked with rotting jute—which I initially think is human hair, causing me to recoil when I brush against the walls. There are four bunks crammed into this tiny space, separated by wood pillars that support the slanted metal roof. The mattresses smell like mould, having been left to weather the snow and then the spring. The wood smells like winter melting into the summer season. We smell like fresh meat.

"We" is me, Robin, Sydney, and Emma, four of the five new housekeepers—a very odd foursome, totally mismatched. We're all young white women, but that's as far as the similarities go. Sydney is small and ginger-haired, with a set of smudged glasses and an exceptionally foul mouth; Robin is broad and strong and quiet, with long black braids; Emma is skinny and coltish and very blonde and very nervous; I'm a bottle redhead and think I'm city slick, but am secretly chewing the insides of my cheeks as I size up my roommates. From what I can glean from grunted conversation on the train and in the air base, we come from different cities and different backgrounds, and we all kind of have different ideas of what we want this summer to be. I sigh, look around at what we're dealing with. While the front girls cabin is sunny and big, this cabin is like the hut in the woods in every scary story I've ever read.

"Ah, fuck," Sydney murmurs, and with that expletive heralding the beginning of our summer, we move in—unceremoniously dragging our duffel bags, leaving snail trails in the dust. I'm stuffed into the top-left bunk; Sydney's below me. On the other side, Emma takes top and Robin claims bottom. This means that Emma and I are almost sleeping side by side in what is basically a plywood double bed—the only things that separate our two mattresses are our bug nets and a low wooden ledge.

And then there's the mess, the artifacts left over from the legions of housekeepers from years prior: trashy gossip magazines, damp pages turning to mush and rotting into the wooden chairs around a rickety table; old sneakers caked with mud and God knows what else; bug-bite lotion; literally hundreds of tampons strewn around the table and the floor, which is very strange and also funny in its overkill. I can sense the spirits of the other young women who came here before me, and it gives me an itchy feeling up and down the backs of my legs and across my palms. Something about the idea of sleeping where so many others have slept makes me feel like I don't quite fit in my own skin—I can feel these ghost girls' pheromones, their frustrations, the exhalations of their dreams still lingering in the high corners of the peaked ceiling.

Four girls slotted into four little wooden bunks. Four bug nets strung up like bridal veils. Four sets of hands at work, throwing old magazines and tampons into garbage bags. Four pairs of feet trudging back and forth to open the door, close the door, open the window, find the broom, find the dustpan, work to make the cabin slightly less inhospitable and just a tiny bit more livable. Four strange, fragile hearts, still alien to one another, beating quickly and wondering how we're going to survive the next nine weeks, cheek to velvety cheek, fingertips to haunches, hip to groin.

* * *

Jack wiggles his eyebrows and laughs, folding his arms and slouching his body in an insouciant way, and the rest of the men follow his lead in an almost spooky manner. There are only two new male staff members, but they are already sniggering along with the veteran guys. The churlish ease of brotherhood makes it simple to adopt a vocabulary of familiarity, and I'm immediately jealous.

The guys are a motley crew. From the way Jack acts—tossing off unofficial orders peppered with insults from the side of his mouth, walking in and out of the crowd with the ease of someone who knows his power and is confident in it—he's the group's natural leader. He's oddly arranged, arresting to glance at but stranger the longer you stare. There's something about the way he holds himself that makes me nervous, and even the way he's built—slump-shouldered and slightly pot-bellied but skinny-armed; bronze-skinned, with his nose peeling from sun exposure; wide-mouthed and all gummy—is new to me, and totally unsettling. Pea, our head dockhand, is the other alpha of the group: his real name is Luke, but it seems that everyone who's worked with him before calls him Pea, short for Sweetpea, because, as Alex leans over to tell me as we watch Pea consider different sizes of ball caps, he's so kind. He's white, sharp-jawed and on the short side, but built like a gymnast, with ropey arms and muscled shoulders. I can't tell what the top half of his face looks like because he has a baseball hat firmly on his head. Then there's Kevin, a fishing guide colloquially known as Kev, or Rook (short for Rookie, from his first year at the lodge), who has pretty doe eyes and ruffled blond hair, a thick and sturdy chest. There's Gus, a veteran guide from Moose Factory—he's tall and broad, Cree, craggy-faced, has deep smile lines around his mouth. There's Pete, a white man in his late fifties, one of the true veteran fishing guides who's been working here since before all the young bucks.

The new male staff members are Aidan and Connor, two dockhands both in their early twenties. Connor, who I flew in with, is from Moose Factory like Gus, and is Cree. So far, all I can tell about him is that he's quiet, one of those people who uses words only when they're really needed. Aidan, a little slow on the uptake, is a tall and oddly mannered white guy from Guelph, with thick, expressive eyebrows and a dark shock of hair. There will also be other men who come and go throughout the season, fishing guides who are flown in for a few weeks at a time but don't want to spend their entire summer here.

So this is the core group; these are the men I'll try to work alongside every day. Nothing about these guys intimidates me right off the bat. I run my eyes over them, assessing body parts, the variances in height, the angle of each neck, the wideness of each stance. Already, from these few visual cues, I can tell a lot about each of them. And if I'm being honest with myself, the idea of sharing my summer—my close quarters, my thoughts, my life for the next few months—with a bunch of young women is scarier than these cocksure young men. These boys could probably become the annoying older brothers I never had. With girls, it could go either way; we could become a coven, or we could turn on one another. Sometimes I find it hard to interact with other women, don't seem to be able to say the right thing. But I want this summer to be different. I want to create sisters. I shove my hands into the pockets of my jeans and cross my fingers as the girls line up.

There's Alex and Tiff, our two superiors. Alex is lean and rangy and full of energy. When I first stepped off the plane, she was in full work mode, already directing housekeepers to cabins with one arm and holding a handful of Thermoses with the other. Tiff is an astrophysics major with a tendency to ask startlingly naive questions. I'm not sure what to make of her. She seems kind, and there's something comforting about her soft-spoken nature, but she's wearing mascara, which strikes me as odd for the middle of nowhere, in a place where no other woman has makeup on, especially not this early in the morning.

Then there's Alisa; she's little and blonde and comes from a fishing family: her grandfather Max has worked here as a fishing guide for years—and will be flying up for a few weeks this summer—and her father is a fisherman back in Southern Ontario.

Most of the housekeepers are new, though: Aubrey, Alex's friend from home, who has giant blue-green eyes and a deter-mined look on her face. Sydney; Robin; Emma. And me.

• • •

At nearly twenty-three years old, I'm one of the oldest girls on staff. And while many of my co-workers either have experience working as fishing and hunting guides or tree trimmers or in aquaculture, or are completing their diplomas in outdoor edu-cation, I'm between the first and second year of trying to finish my master of fine arts in creative writing at the University of British Columbia. It's not an easy program to get into, and rattling off the name of my degree usually gets me some form of respect. Here, however, the ability to write a novel is pitiful compared with the ability to split firewood or tie a proper knot or identify a bird just from its flight pattern. Here, my writing degree means nearly nothing.

When I was getting ready to move out west, everyone told me that once I'd settled in to Vancouver, I'd never want to leave.

Once I got to Vancouver, all I wanted to do was go. The city was brutal: my first month there, I didn't realize that there were mountains because the weather was so shitty that the fog occluded everything. For the first six weeks, I didn't see the sun, because I had moved during Vancouver's worst and rainiest autumn of the past decade. For the first three months, I battled a bedbug infestation that came with my trendy Kitsilano apartment. For the first half of the year, I cried hard and often: on the bus, in my hot yoga class, in my shower. Vancouver was my first time living on my own in a big city. I had pictured independence, writing dates in coffee shops, lots of laughter with new friends—all of the typical girl-moves-away-from-home clichés. Instead, there was an intense kind of loneliness that came from being halfway across the country from my family and in a different time zone; from being one of the youngest in my program, not at all experienced in life like my classmates were; from sitting alone in my apartment, with the damp of the rain in the air and all of my clothes bundled into giant plastic bags to protect them from the bedbugs I was trying to eradicate.

Nine months on, Vancouver is still an enemy: I hate the rain, I hate the slow walkers, I hate how expensive it is, and, most of all, I hate the idea of buckling down for the next year and editing my thesis, a novel that my adviser, from what I can tell, despises with all his heart.

Summer planning was easy when I was at my desk in my apartment in downtown Vancouver, on the grid and plugged in. But standing here, overtired and bleary, I'm not sure why I chose to do this. This is what happens when someone feels confident behind a computer screen, applying for a job she really doesn't know anything about because the idea of being physically worked to the bone for nine weeks seems more appealing than the grind of writing a thesis, chasing down my adviser, trying to keep up with his haphazard and temperamental edits. This is what happens when a master's student is so fed up with her program that she wants to get away for a break at any cost. When I was warned by Henry in his preliminary staff emails that there might be snowstorms up here, even in May, I figured it was better than weeks of never-ending rain wearing on me, compounding the anxiety I was feeling about maybe not graduating on time. When I was told that there wouldn't be any internet or cellphone service, I thought that was better than sending my adviser email after panicked email. When I realized that Kesagami would be a challenge, that I'd be exhausted and worked hard and completely out of my comfort zone, I figured I could handle it.

* * *

"Anna." Alex is holding out a ball cap: it's deep green, with the Kesagami branding across the front. I smile and grab it.

When we all pull on our matching uniforms and line up in front of Henry for the first time this season, I can finally easily tell the vets from the newbies. The veterans' shirts are bleached around the collars from the sun, the material faded and comfortable-looking. My shirt is fresh out of the package, dark green and itchy. My new hat sits funny on my head, its brim not yet moulded by hot hands. Despite the discrepancies, we're all part of the same machine: when I covertly glance up and down the line of us, standing shoulder to shoulder, I realize how similar we look. We're lanky, jumpy, filled with a weird energy; some of us pull our hats low to cover our dark-circled eyes, moving with a startling similarity; some of us smack our gum, popping and cracking like our tired bones; our shirts are all cut the same way, so curves and hips and gender and posture are almost hidden underneath the bright yellow writing that marks out our life for the next sixty-odd days: *Kesagami Lodge Staff*.

Henry launches into a speech that is supposed to put verve into our spines, though we're all too tired to care. As he speaks about the summer to come, about knowing our place and not fraternizing with the guests and working the hardest we possibly can, I assess the differences I see in him between this year and last. As a lodge manager interacting with guests, Henry was obsequious in the way that people who have worked years in customer service become. As a manager interacting with his staff, he has an edge of granite. Henry's an interesting study in contrasts: he wears the utilitarian quick-dry gear of fishermen, as if he could go out onto the water to get messy at any moment, but his khaki-coloured shirt and pants are absolutely spotless. He's been up for a few days already, but there's not a salt-and-pepper hair out of place on his head. He's well put together and talks in a measured, metronomic way, and at the same time, there's something coiled about him.

His speech is met with our slouches, our half-shut eyes, our slow, dumb breathing. Many of us haven't been broken in; I'm one of them. A bunch of us are kind of smug, kind of slick. I turn my head and look beyond our lineup, to the west windows, to the trees swaying slightly in the wind. I imagine the land as party to our smugness, crossing its arms and staring, snickering at us through the grubby dining room windows and beneath the cracks of the doors. *Just wait*, it murmurs, showing teeth made of pike bones and Jack pine bark. *You'll learn.*

*　　*　　*

The first night in the back cabin, the four of us don't stay up to chat. Instead, we lie in our bunks, silent and still. When I shift my gaze upward, I see that the names of all the female employees who have lived in this cabin throughout the years are written on the ceiling in permanent marker, along with inside jokes, nicknames, their coded wishes and hopes and upsets— all there, quiet graffiti watching over the rookies. I try not to think about the people who came before me; instead, I shift around on my mouldy mattress, listening to the other women. I'm pretty sure all of us are lying awake, trying to slow our breathing to make it sound like we're slipping into sleep. But none of us is; we're not even close. I'm thinking about my choices, what led me here, what led these other women here. What we might be running away from. What I'm running into. The fauna. The flora. The forest behind me, looming outside the little window at my head. The branches are just a few inches too short to tap against the glass; they fold and sway with the wind, casting shapes on my pillow. Every crack, rustle, lick of the wind makes my eyes fly open, but I don't have the guts to lift my head, turn around, and peer out the window into the darkness.

I lie there for a long time. My thoughts race; mostly I feel worried, a greasy knot in my gut. It's entirely possible that I've made a gigantic mistake, sacrificing my privacy, my body, maybe even my sanity for these sixty-seven days. Still, the fluttering breathing of three other worried souls surrounds me, almost soothes me. Somehow, already, I feel vaguely connected to these women, we, the new ones, relegated to a falling-apart hut, sent to the woods. Already, the four of us are absorbing one another's pheromones, idiosyncrasies, fears, and desires. Desire that the summer will give us what we need—except not all of us know what we need, and most of us have no idea what we want. But we've thrown our lot to the North, and all we can do now is hope that the North reciprocates.

Eventually, I fall into a patchy, grey-tinged sleep, and in what seems like only a few minutes, I wake up to an even more grey-tinged morning, all of our alarms going off at the same time, Sydney throwing on her clothes, pale flesh flashed in clammy strips, Robin swearing across a muzzy tongue, Emma caught in her bug net as she tries to roll out of her bunk and land without clipping Robin.

I sit straight up in my bed, panicked from confusion about where I am. I see the boys strolling by our cabin on their way to breakfast, blatantly trying to look in our front window to see our body parts as we change.

"What time is it?" My voice is crappy with sleep; I can tell that my mouth smells like rot.

"Six o'fucking clock," Sydney growls, punching the air in a low jab.

Jack stands outside our cabin, staring in, laughing at us, Pea looking over his shoulder with a grin. I watch, exhausted, as Jack picks up a handful of gravel and throws it into the air.

I'm confused until the rocks hit our roof with an unholy clatter. We all shriek.

His yell echoes as he walks down the path to breakfast: "Welcome to the summer, assholes!"

QUEEN OF FISHES

The morning of our first real day of work, we sit around in the dining room, feeling one another out. The standard questions are asked: How old are you? What's your background? Where are you from? Most of the workers come from towns with interesting names—Moose Factory, Lion's Head, Skead, Thornloe. There are a few people from places that I immediately recognize: Orangeville, Belleville, London, Guelph. And then there's me, the only person from a metropolis.

When it's my turn, I mumble that metropolis under my breath.

"What?" Jack hoots.

"Toronto," I repeat.

Then Jack and Pea and Kev and Gus do this odd coordinated thing, where they all click the fat of their tongues and smile weird, predator grins.

"Shit, girl," Gus says. "That's the first strike against you."

I know it is. This is one of those markers that make me the resident interloper. There are others: I go to writing school, not an outdoor-adventure education program. I'm older than the majority of the housekeepers, though I'm still barely an adult and definitely not yet a woman. And last year—improbably, surprisingly, wonderfully—I was a guest at the lodge. I slept in one of the beds that I'm going to make every morning; I ate the food that I'm going to be serving to impatient guests; and I got to walk down the dock, got to sling myself into a boat and jet across the lake all day, every day. Best of all, I got to hold a fishing rod in my hand and trawl the water for the great, fierce beauties that lurk beneath the surface—the treasured beasts that are northern pike.

• • •

My father started fishing at Kesagami fifteen years ago, and while my younger brother joined him for the occasional father-son fishing trip, I said no every time I was asked to come along. It wasn't that I had never fished before: my father started us young in the city, my brother and I learning how to catch gleaming little sunfish and bass in Toronto's High Park using sturdy Mickey Mouse fishing rods, goofy red-and-white bobbers, and worms that we always made Dad put on the hook because we weren't brave enough to spear a living thing with steel. But as I got older, I wanted to spend less time sitting still on a shoreline and more time being a moody preteen, and then a moody teenager. I wanted to spend my summer weeks in backyard pools, or at illicit parents-out-of-town house parties, or lying on my bed using ICQ to see if I could chat with whoever my crush was that week. As a teenager, the idea of five or six or seven days away from the internet and my friends and the telephone and the heat of a good, sticky Toronto summer was unappealing. And then, as I got older, life got busier, and I couldn't justify taking a week off work to float around in a boat for eight hours a day. I wanted hustle and bustle, and so the thought of Northern Ontario became more than just unappealing—it became terrifying. Why walleye guts? Why bears? Why uncomfortable beds? Why fishermen? Why silence out on the middle of a lake? I didn't understand, and I didn't think I ever would.

And then, when I was in the first year of my undergraduate degree, my uncle died.

Uncle Pete wasn't technically my uncle. He was my father's cousin. Pete and his wife, Sue, had two sons who were just a bit older than me and my brother, and so when all of us were younger, and we were more fun and less hampered by personality and geography, there were lots of trips back and forth across the border to Ohio where they lived. We were wild kind-of cousins wrestling, or jumping from bunk bed to bunk bed, or just lying beside one another on the floor, whispering about nothing the way children do. We were different, lived in different places, and had different points of view, different temperaments—and, as we got older, different beliefs—but when we were together, we were blood.

Sometimes blood stays with you for a long time, thick and comforting and keeping you afloat. Sometimes we lose people before we think we will. One night, I was sitting at my desk in my university dormitory, sketching out some notes for an English essay, when I got a phone call. Uncle Pete had died of a heart attack at the age of fifty-five, and my aunt had found his body on the bathroom floor.

I remember crying at my desk. And I remember, a few months later, my father coming up with an idea: sometime in the future, we were going to go on a family fishing trip to celebrate Pete. Our two families grew close, grew apart, came back together again, caught and fissured and held in the sheer grief of losing a patriarch, a cousin, an uncle. A loved one.

And that's how, only a year ago, four years after Uncle Pete had died, I found myself wedged into a minivan with my cousins, starting on the drive to the tiny Cochrane air base to go up to Kesagami. Seven of us went all in; we fell. I spent my mornings slotted into one of the distinctive green boats with some combination of cousins, uncle, father, brother, as hours trickled by in amiable silence; we spent our afternoons eating fresh-fried fish, weathering the rain, speeding back to shore to curl up around the fireplaces.

When we went out fishing, ghosts tagged along. It was hard not to believe in spirits while witnessing the formidable nature of our environment, while skimming across the surface of the lake, while trying to outrun a huge thunderstorm, motor gunned and guide laughing, swigging cans of beer and opening our mouths to the coming rain. It wasn't hard to believe that Uncle Pete was there with us, large and jolly, propped up in the back of the boat, cheering us on with his giant, jocular laugh. I'm sure he watched his sons. And he made sure that we caught what we needed to catch.

One morning, I was out with my father and my brother, trawling for walleye. It was a grey-velour day: the water and the sky and the clouds were all the same colour, and the air was so still that the surface of the lake was like concrete-coloured glass. So still that I could hear the giggled conversations going on in the other family boats. So still that I didn't notice at first that there was something tugging truculently on the other end of my line.

That weight. I had never felt a weight like that. All of my fish up until that point had been walleye, smaller and wriggly. But this was a ballast, this was an unseen thing, something maw-mouthed dragging idly on my pink twister jig. "Stickfish," my father said—a stick hooked to my line, a result of my tendency to jig too deep because of a lack of experience. But I knew it wasn't a stick. This wasn't flora. It felt thicker; there was a ripple of awareness on the other end of the line. An opponent. A presence. An intelligence.

The longest time in the world is from when you have a fish on until when you manage to get that fish into the boat. I wasn't jigging with a leader, a piece of wire that people use to prevent toothy fish from biting off a hook, so I knew that if it was a pike I had on the other end, it could easily snap my line off. I stood and I reeled, one rotation at a time, a novice in all regards but so focused on this one task that the gentle hoots and catcalls of my family teasing me sounded as if they were coming from far away. I thought about the way the horizon and lake were bleeding into each other, listened to the slap of the water against the side of the boat. Felt the heaviness. Two beasts facing off from opposite ends of a thin thread, each wondering about the other, each unsure of the other end of the line. I called on all my spirits in that one moment, praying to any god, to the crows, to the bears, to the lake itself, to my future, to anyone and anything that would take pity on me. Praying to my uncle. Praying to my family.

And something—someone—listened, because I brought that pike to the surface.

*   *   *   *

Pike: otherwise known as northerns, jackfish, slough sharks, hammer handles, dragons, torpedoes, toothies, snot rockets, slime darts, snake pickerel, slimers, slime snakes, leader shredders, junk fish. When you're fishing for bass and get your line bit off: "Those fucking pike," the refrain hissed by fishermen throughout the centuries, and members of my family more than once or twice. When you've travelled across the continent to Northern Ontario to fish specifically for these cranky beauties: "Those fucking pike," murmured in awe at their slyness, their gravitas.

At Kesagami, pike are the main feature, the beast that everyone chases. Worthy opponents; watchful predators; sneaky bastards. *Esox lucius*: water wolves.

But fishing for these cranky beauties isn't a chore; nobody really swears under their breath if they hook into a big one by accident. Up here, fishing for pike becomes a kind of meditation. There's a moment of spirituality in being alone on a lake as silent and giant as this. There's something sacred about staring into water that is deep and dark and quiet—our original font, the ooze from which we all crawled at one point—without knowing what exactly is staring back at you.

At the same time, pike are beautiful. It might seem odd to call one of Canada's most prolific carnivorous fish pretty, but they are. Pike are most often olive green, with a pearlescent, pale belly and gold stripes or spots marking their flanks. Add in reddish fins, and a bright northern sun, and pulling a pike from the water can be prismatic, a peacocky experience.

Elsewhere, pike have been identified as pests. Conservation efforts for these fish don't always catch on: the bigger the teeth, the less human empathy a species garners, and pike aren't what anyone would deem "cute"—after all, when it comes down to it, wolves don't make good pets. Some experts deem pike an invasive species—if pike manage to make it into a body of water they're not natural to, they tend to cause destruction by eating all the other fish (and even each other).

I had never really thought about pike before. I had heard my father talk about them in reverent tones; I had seen photos of his biggest catches; I knew that they existed, that they were fighters, that people seemed to either love or hate them. How could I revere the predators on land, the animals that continue to hook artists' imaginations and create space for themselves in people's consciousnesses, and yet ignore the ancients that, cloaked in lake, went under the radar? Pike are ancient fish. For a while, it was believed that *E. lucius* got its start in northern Eurasia, and that it evolved from *Palaeoesox fritschei*, back in 60 million BCE. A 1980 discovery of a sixty-million-year-old pike skeleton in Western Canada, however, put the boots to that theory. Now scientists believe that pike in North America evolved separately from Eurasia—that the Eurasian variety was a warm-water pike, and that the North American pike were of two types: first, the muskellunge, commonly abbreviated as the muskie, and then the cold-water pike. But you don't really need a scientist to tell you about how primordial these fish are; you only have to pull a pike out of the water, its thick body writhing and thrashing, to see its heritage; you only have to look at the dinosaur-snouted faces, the wicked-eyed stares, the bodies the colour of foliage to understand why fishermen—like my father, who has two four-foot fibreglass trophy-pike replicas mounted in our family home—deem them such worthy challengers.

Throughout history, these fish have evoked divisive feelings; this is a creature with a complicated, rich mythology, and examining its written history shows that. The first reference to pike—*Lucius*—comes from fourth-century Roman poet Decimus Magnus Ausonius in "Mosella," his poem written about the river Moselle: "Lucius besieges the complaining frogs / in obscure holes among sedges and mud. / His meat is not for the dining table / but sold at cheap shops smoky with its reeking stink." Another early reference to pike comes from a poem by Geoffrey Chaucer. He mentions it in one of his love poems, "To Rosemounde"— *"Nas neuer pyk walwed in galauntyne* (Never was pike so imbued in galantine [sauce]) / *As I in love am walwed and ywounde* (As I in love, am imbued and wounded)"—romance at its finest. *The Compleat Angler*, a treatise on the joys of fishing, by Izaak Walton, was published in 1653, and then added to and edited by the writer for the next twenty-five years. The pike "is to be taken the tyrant, as the Salmon is the king, of the fresh water . . . the fresh-water wolf, by reason of his bold, greedy, devouring disposition. . . . A man going to a pond . . . to water his mule, had a Pike bit his mule by the lips, to which the Pike hung fast."

It's rare that pike are described as fish to be admired or revered: instead, they're eaten, feared, avoided. They're lurking in ponds and waiting for unwitting prey; they're on tables as a second thought. And all of this seems unfair to me, as someone who's grappled with these fish and prayed to be able to catch one. Other predators have been given respect throughout history. Why not this one?

I look to the folklore to figure it out. The stories that surround the northern pike give a glimpse into the dichotomous beliefs that these fish evoke. Russian mythology dictates that the pike can be a bad water-spirit, or a wise old wish-fulfiller. A piece of apocrypha has Theodoric the Great, an Ostrogoth king, dying of shock and grief in 526 AD when the markings on the head of a large fish—reportedly a pike—served at his dinner table resembled the face of an enemy he had recently killed. In *The Once and Future King*, an Arthurian fantasy novel, young King Arthur narrowly avoids being eaten by a giant moat pike. And while fish such as sturgeon and salmon play important roles in Anishinaabe legends, the pike doesn't appear too often; if it does, it's cast as a bogeyman or a lake monster, or a fish that someone has turned into only to avoid the fate of drowning. Some general mythology even has pike eating hapless fishermen, becoming the "king of the fishes" in this ultimate act of domination.

A pike's frightening features and personality only add to its allure for fishermen. Pike have good vision, and their eyeballs are mobile; they can easily track speed and judge depth and distance. Their jaws click when they close; their teeth are designed to hold and destroy: sharp dentary teeth on the bottom jaw to pierce the skin of prey, and tooth pads on the roof of the mouth to trap that prey and keep it from escaping. Esocid teeth are extremely sharp, which accounts for why pike can roll their big heads and snap off that fishing line—"leader shredders." It also means that pike bites bleed but good; some fishermen will tell you it's rumoured that pike have an anticoagulant in their saliva, so if you're out on a lake and get nailed by one of these fish, your day is probably done.

And, of course, size factors into it. While nowhere near as large as a grouper or a marlin, a catfish or a sturgeon, the pike's dimensions are nothing to sniff at. A three-year-old northern pike has an average length of about nineteen inches, while adults can grow to four feet or more. The heaviest pike on record weighed 55.1 pounds, and was caught in Germany in 1986; the Ontario record for a northern pike is 42.12 pounds, caught near Kenora in 1946. But weight is not the only measure of a pike: a skinnier pike that is long and strong can still wreak havoc on a fishing line, and while length seems to be less important in the annals of pike-fishing history, some of the biggest northerns at Kesagami clock in at about fifty inches, with the longest being rumoured at fifty-five inches.

Pike are even more impressive in action. To strike, they lie in wait and then burst toward their prey at maximum acceleration—they form an S-shape with their thick bodies, and then snap forward by quickly straightening out, keeping their mouths closed until the last possible moment in order to build up a vacuum and suck unwitting targets into their gullets. Their aim is not always true, but the action of a pike strike is daunting and dynamic, and can be seen on the surface of the water in what is called the swirl. From where you stand in a boat, hunched over and staring into the water, beseeching, the swirl almost looks like a boiling sign of infinity, a perfect taunt: *I've been here for years, and I'll be here for years more.* This is why so many people fish for pike: to see the strike adds to the excitement and the fear.

And then there's the fight. It seems fitting that pike get their name from the resemblance they bear to the medieval pole weapon. Think about the fight that a four-foot-long fish with a wolf's instincts might give you. First, there's setting the hook: pike are bony. Because they're so hard-mouthed, an angler needs to set the hook hard and properly—snapping the rod back at the exact right time once the fish hits the lure to try to bury the hook in the jawbone (ideal) or flesh (less ideal)—in order to keep the northern on the line, which, it must be said, is no easy feat. I've heard of pike getting hooked and then immediately adjusting course to dive back under the boat, to waste line and make it more difficult for the angler to reel them in.

In this day and age, as tackle gets more and more complicated and garish, there's something primordial and powerful about fishing with simple gear, with a single, barbless hook. The fight becomes fair; the pike get a chance. To catch the pike fairly, judiciously, and beautifully, we have to become the pike. We have to reach into that part of us that remembers. We have to tap into our ancient instincts, stare into that impenetrable water, and cast our line without knowing what will be waiting for us on the other end.

Malevolent, bold, greedy, devouring, reeking tyrant—this is our angry lupine water hunter, the wolf that lies in wait to bite off indolent, dangling fingers or thirsty mules' lips, to eat a stupid fisherman who makes just one misstep. No daydreaming with hands in the water where pike live and breed, if the literature is to be believed. No interloping in a pike's domain. We can only bow to the ruler.

*　*　*

When I pulled my pike up, my brother and father hanging over the side of the boat with the cradle at the ready, I thought she was dead because she was so calm. She didn't come up swirling or thrashing. She didn't fight me. Instead, she floated to the boat on her side, her one visible eye focused steadily on us. The lure was hooked lightly in her cheek; one twist and that fish could have gotten away—but she didn't. Instead, she stared at me, and I stared back. She was thirty-six inches. Not a huge pike, but not a small one either. I was awed at how she came in so slowly, lackadaisical, pulled along by my lurid bait; at the gleaming patterns on her back of sinews and slime—deep green and browns, brindled patches of gold and beige; at her pale belly; at the hazel and black irises; at the sentient gaze.

Before we returned her to the water, holding her by the tail and letting her slowly re-aerate her gills, I put my bare hand on her back. I should have been wearing a glove, to prevent my skin from removing necessary mucus from her skin, but I couldn't help it. This was sheer power and patience beneath my palm. My hand came away covered in slickness, and I put it to my face, smelled the brackish brown water on my skin, the life of a fish. And then my pike was lowered into the water, and my pike was gone.

Pike break your heart. Pike make you stronger. They have sneakily, sensually captured our imaginations: "A pike dozed," Amy Lowell writes. "Green and copper, / A darkness and a gleam." "With one sinuous ripple," Theodore Roethke describes in the finale of a poem, "then a rush / A thrashing up of the whole pool." These are fish that have seen the deaths of kings, eaten lips of mules, besieged the fisherman. These are eyes that have seen the fillet knife, the faces of excited and frustrated anglers. For all of this, the pike deserves more credit than we've given it. Water wolf. Survivor in the fullest. This queen of fishes.

PIN BONES

On our second day as Kesagami staff, Alex and Tiff take the new housekeepers around camp once again, this time showing us how to clean the motel rooms, bathrooms, bathhouse, cabins— or rather, how to clean as fast as we can without putting too much elbow grease into it.

"Here's your secret weapon," Alex says, slamming a spray bottle full of blue liquid onto the cheap plastic patio table in the middle of Cabin 3.

"Windex?" Emma cranes her head to look at the label.

"Windex," she affirms. "Well, off-brand Windex, so it's not as good and also might be more toxic. Make sure you dilute it. But yeah, basically Windex."

"Kesagami rule number one: use only what you need to use," Tiff chimes in from across the cabin. "Windex works for pretty much everything. We even use it to clean the toilet bowls."

Getting the lodge ready for the guests in only a few days isn't easy. In some previous years, the winter was so harsh that the entire dock was ripped apart and set sail across the lake during the spring thaw. Sometimes, wildlife has been found nesting in the cabins. One year, a marten destroyed Henry's bedroom; another year, chipmunks inhabited the guideshack and had to be systematically killed throughout the summer.

The damage this year isn't bad. The dock is still present; no rodent has chewed the electrical wiring in the lodge to bits; the roof is intact; the shoreline hasn't been torn up by ice. Jack and Pea, who came up a few days earlier than the rest of us to start the opening procedures, found a groundhog living in the guide-shack and used chicken wire and a staple gun to pen it into Kevin's bunk, but that seems to be the extent of the mayhem.

Still, there's a lot to be done before the first guests fly in. All of the linens need to be pulled out of storage and washed; dishes need to be dusted off and bleached and rinsed and stacked on their shelves; all of the rooms and cabins need to be unlocked and opened and aired. Tables need to be polished, floors vacuumed, counters wiped down, windows scrubbed, paths swept, and leaves raked. Already, we've been moving and stacking wood, dragging furniture around, unpacking bottles of liquor, and displaying Kesagami T-shirts to sell to guests as souvenirs, setting up mattresses and pillows and shaking out duvets, filling the fridge with the groceries that were flown in with us and continue to be delivered by plane.

Elsewhere, the dockhands and guides are busy at the shoreline. Their main task is bringing the boats out of storage where they've been kept all winter in the narrows, a part of the lake about a ten-minute boat ride away where the water goes into a kind of strait. There's more shelter there, and so it's where Henry chooses to store the boats in the off-season.

The boys have the job of towing the freight canoes back to the main shoreline and getting them into their rails, which are peeled black spruce trees nailed together along the shoreline like latticework, a structure designed to keep a boat steady and held tight and safe, out of the lake. Once the big canoes are docked and ready, the guides and dockhands set up boat seats and cushions, organize tackle boxes, chop firewood, stain cabin decks, clean chimneys, drag picnic tables to prime positions.

The work has been constant and fast, and our learning curves have been steep. All the new staff members are covered in scratches and bruises and smudges of dirt, battered by an unfamiliar environment that we don't quite understand. The labour is already wreaking havoc on my body, which is used to doing desk jobs and sitting on buses and subways, not lifting and hauling and scrubbing over and over again. My triceps are tight and painful; my fingertips are chapped; my lower back feels like something has popped out and needs to be smacked back in. And I'm tired. I'm so tired I feel like I could sleep twelve hours tonight and still sleep some more. Every cell in my body is crying out for more rest. Waking up this morning felt like tearing through a thick grey screen; my head has been aching all day long as a result of the 6 a.m. alarm. I have to believe this is only an adjustment, that after a few weeks my body will become tight and strong and I'll get used to the repetitive motions that are causing me such grief, but right now, everything is tender. I'm dumb-headed and thick-brained, more of a hindrance than a help. I feel out of place and fragile, and I wonder why I ever wanted to come up here.

Tiff leans over one of the beds, showing us how to change the sheets and master a hospital corner while dodging the spiders that live in the jute. On the other side of the cabin, Alex sweeps the hearth of the fireplace. "Just make sure that all the ashes are cold," she says over her shoulder to us, "because we've had a few experiences where girls have put live coals into plastic buckets."

Suddenly, there's a terrible bang, and everything goes dark. I stand stock-still, wondering what the hell has happened. I hear Tiff sigh and walk a few steps, and then the watery cabin light is flicked on and I see that the door has been slammed shut.

"What the fuck?" The new girls start to froth, panicked, but Alex, Tiff, and Alisa lean back against the bunks, picking at their nails and their split ends.

"It's the guys," Alisa says. "They do this all the time when we're cleaning."

That's when I notice low guffaws from outside the door. I run up to it and try the handle, but it's locked: the cabin doors lock both from the inside and the outside. There's more laughter.

I look back at the veteran housekeepers, bewildered. "So what now?"

"It's an excuse not to do work," Tiff says with a smile, lying down on one of the bunks. "It's not like we can get outside, anyway."

"So you let them do this?"

"Yeah," Alex says.

"Are you kidding me?" I stare at them, probably looking like an idiot who thinks she knows it all. Tiff's and Alex's eyebrows go up.

I hit the heel of my palm against the glass of one of the rusted, reticent windows, and slide it open, forcing the panes along their dirty tracks. Luckily, there's a firewood box underneath the window that provides a step down, so I manage to escape, albeit in a graceless tumble. In the process, I slice my shin open on the frame. When I hit the ground, the boys hear me: they crane their heads around the edge of the cabin, while behind me, the girls poke their heads out of the window.

I walk around to the door and unlatch it, trying to stop the flow of blood from my leg with a useless cupped hand. Jack looks at me, inscrutable. Kev grins. The girls' faces are all white in the sunlight when the door swings open.

"Fuck you," I say, over my shoulder and loudly, the words juicy in my mouth, and I'm not entirely sure who I'm saying them to.

* * *

The work continues, non-stop, for three days. In that time, we hand-wash every pot, pan, and cooking implement in the kitchen. We scrub every toilet bowl and wipe every mirror. Every bed is made with freshly cleaned sheets, every pillow plumped, every roll of toilet paper carefully placed on the holder with the first square folded into a neat little triangle.

We also fill the woodlots with sliced and diced chunks of black spruce. I can tell that wood is going to be our main commodity. It already seems to be in motion constantly: moving from place to place, being stacked and restacked. If Henry doesn't like where one woodpile is, he makes us move it. If he decides he doesn't like the change, we move it back. He's always thinking about where is best to stack wood, how best to stack wood, where the wood will be best seasoned and protected from the elements—which seems futile to me, because our entire tract of land is at the mercy of those elements.

We move the wood. We restack the piles. We chap our palms, bruise our elbows and knees, get splinters in our fingers. We work until we can't carry another armful of spruce, and then we wake up the next morning and do it all over again.

The staff fishing day is the reward for our labour. It's a yearly tradition for the lodge employees—a day on the water to relax before the guests arrive. One day when we get to experience what the guests get to experience every day. One day when we get to scud across the lake in those big deep-green boats and try our luck at getting a bite.

We're grateful when our fishing morning comes clear and beautiful, a contrast to the overcast days we've been toiling through so far. The sky is a giant canvas of blue, ready for the paint of the sun, and I can sense the heat that will herald the start of the summer weather. We tumble down the dock in old gumboots and windbreakers borrowed from the lodge closets. The girls stand at the edge of the dock and bare our teeth at one another, mock-jostling as we line up to snag a berth in the boat we most want, cranking our heads back as we sun our necks and cheeks in focused pleasure. The guides idle and wait for us as we pile into the rocking boats. I end up with Syd, and Tiff and Jack, who are our resident couple on staff. I'm wary of Jack, but Tiff and Syd seem fun and sweet, and I trust them to make this day the best it can be. Pea's boat has Alex, Alisa, and Aubrey; Kevin has Robin, Connor, and Emma; Pete has Aidan;

and Gus, Sam, and Henry make up the boat of adults. It's interesting to observe the divisions: obviously Tiff will pair up with Jack when she can, and Alex and Alisa are veterans, so they want to be together; Kevin has the boat of random new people; and Aidan has been shunted off with Pete because none of the younger guides wants to deal with his constant questions and odd anecdotes.

And then we're roaring across the lake, no care for speed or safety, no second thoughts for life jackets or tying our hair back to protect from wind-tangle. Our five boats jet out across the water like green arrows, and I think *this is freedom* and I know I have to drink this up, because this one morning in the shimmer of the bold northern sunlight is all I'm going to have this summer in terms of experiencing this lake in all its guts and glory and guile. After this, as Henry has made clear, the female workers are bound to the shore, stuck doing laundry and making beds and mopping floors. After this, we're grounded.

When we reach a respectable distance from shore, we strip down to bikini strings and bare shoulders; I collect insect bodies across my collarbones, their fragile wings snared in my sunscreen.

"Happy birthday, Jack," Syd says, as he picks the spot where we're going to fish for the morning. He's twenty-five today.

"And what a birthday," he says, tying a Palomar knot on Syd's line, deftly attaching her hook to the filament. *Now make me proud* is the unspoken sentiment. The boats are drafted teams, whether we like it or not, and there's an unspoken competition going on: Who can catch the most fish? Who, therefore, is the most able guide? What boy can best force his housekeepers not to fuck around?

By midmorning, we're in the best kind of trance. The minutes topple into each other, and they're filled with the satisfying nips and jerks of a taut fishing line, a quiet pleasure. There's something about being out on a body of water on a calm, warm day. There's no panic, no thinking about chores to do, no tension between veterans and newbies. Instead, our boats quietly cheer one another on in between a joke here and there. It's as if being away from the shore and the buildings and all the potential stresses those hold has softened our edges; I'm not on the offence, or even the defence. I'm only concentrating on the way the line feels against my right pointer finger, the way Syd is humming to herself behind me, the way the wide brim of Jack's fisherman fedora casts a shadow over the top half of his face, the way Tiff is staring out at the horizon, eyes half-lidded and dreamy.

It's said that the walleye from Kesagami Lake are the sweetest, freshest fish you'll ever taste. I've heard of guests who spent hours getting one walleye strike after another—*bang, bang, bang*—so many that they caught more than two or three hundred fish in a day. And after I catch my first walleye, I undo the hook and kiss the fish right on the cheek, a ritual for rookie fishermen. I like to think of it as thanking the lake for what I'm taking from it.

"Nice one," Jack says, popping the fish into a bucket.

"Do you think we'll catch any pike today?" I don't look at him as I ask.

Jack laughs as he helps Syd unspool a bird's nest she's created around her reel. "You think you're gonna catch a pike?"

I know that I've somehow shown too much, revealed an animal part of my mind that should have stayed hidden. I don't tell him that I already have, I've already felt it, that I want more.

Jack has caught hundreds of pike; Jack knows better than me. I raise one shoulder in lukewarm acquiescence, and it's enough that he turns away, tying another knot.

Kesagami is special in that it's strict cruelty-free fishing: it's all catch and release, save for the walleye the guests are allowed to eat for their daily shore lunch. There are lots of rules about how best to preserve the fish population. Guests use barbless hooks, which means that although the hook may go deeper than a barbed one, unhooking a fish is cleaner and less damaging; when handling pike, guides and guests should wear gloves to protect the mucus on the fish skin; nets aren't allowed, only cradles, because nets bend the fish, but cradles hold them straight and safe in the water. I've been told that pike are a tasty fish, albeit difficult to fillet because they're bony, but here, pike are absolutely never to be killed. I've never heard of a guest killing a pike; I'm sure it would result in a lifetime ban from the lodge. Kesagami is so far north—it's very expensive and not at all convenient to visit—and it's only open for about two months a year, so there's less fishing pressure on the lake. All of these factors combined mean that Kesagami's pike have become known as some of the biggest, canniest pike in North America, if not the world. So as we squeal and joke and jig for walleye and miss setting the hook again and again, I remember that we're fishing on a lake of legends, that somewhere, the pike can hear us, know us, are getting ready to spend the summer alongside us.

· · ·

All of the boats head to one of the islands to set up shore lunch, a meal of deep-fried battered fish and onion rings and potato slices. Fishermen crave shore lunch. The guides have to make it every day they're out on the water, unless their guests ask for a packed lunch in order to get another hour of fishing out of the day. But the housekeepers get to taste fresh-caught fish only this once. It's also going to be the only time the boys will cook for the girls, so we take full advantage. We kneel in the shallows in our bathing suits to cool off as the guides fire up the propane tanks, shoving one another out of the way with their elbows and the heels of their hands.

Jack, in a moment of rare and brilliant patience, tries to teach a few of the girls how to fillet, using the broad end of one of the boat paddles as a cutting board. I watch as Tiff and Robin turn walleye flesh into ragged streamers. When it's my turn, I sit cross-legged on the white sand and hold the Rapala knife awkwardly in one loose-fingered hand.

"Here," he says, taking one of my hands, mechanically, like a shop-class instructor. "Feel *here*."

The fish meat is pearl-coloured. When I put my fingers where Jack guides them, the silky flesh is cool and smooth to the touch. He moves my hand around, looking for something— the way a boy gets his hand under a girl's skirt but keeps his eyes on her face.

"Ah." He's found it. "The pin bones." I struggle to find them, and he sighs, recalibrating my hand. And suddenly, there it is: I feel a ridge in the reams and furrows of slick meat. A line of tiny bones. The pin bones that float, unattached, in the middle of muscle. Bones that are designed to make a fish tense up and swim as far and as fast as possible. They prick my fingers in a plaintive rhythm as I move my hands along their curving pathway.

Jack supervises as I cut the pin bones out of the tattered meat. They're encased in their thin, pale strip of flesh, and for a moment I look at them, the whole outfit opaline in the bright sun. I like the idea of an escape mechanism embedded deep in a body. I stare up at Jack, and his eyes are so green in the sun that they make my head hurt.

Then he grabs the strip and flings it into the water. "Hurry the fuck up."

* * *

On the way back in from shore lunch, Jack throws the motor into full throttle, gunning it, and the other boats catch up in an eddy of sound. He tosses us paddles, and we're close enough to the other boats to see fox-like smiles. Pea's boat is set up, Alex and Alisa dragging their paddles in the water, and as he yanks on the motor, the boat does a sharp turn, and we're soaked in the resulting spray. There are screams. Syd and I struggle with the oars, unsure how to turn them to get the best spray. We accidentally nail Jack and Tiff more than once until we get the hang of it. Tiff guides us through the motions, sitting with her legs slung open, her face determined and shining and her hair whipping around her shoulders, and we learn how to be contenders. The boats drive in glittering doughnuts around one another, the Yamaha motors growling but not loud enough to drown out everyone's wild laughter, and we fight back, aiming at Pea and Kev, holding on and desperately trying not to give in to the drag of wood on water and topple into the lake. The boat with Henry and Sam and Gus is long gone—the adults have left the lake, given up for the day, as if they knew what mischief was impending—and so we let rip.

The feeling of unease and uncertainty that has been sitting cold in my gut since landing starts to unknot itself. The sun is shining, the air smells like spruce and bracken, and the water slices up around our fingertips and faces in shining arcs, wrapping around us and pasting the soft curls of our finest hair to the napes of our necks. I could reach out and feel the spray of a thousand or more drops of water collide with my skin, feel the lake reach back to me—threatening or welcoming, I can't tell—curling its fingers and beckoning, murmuring, holding the rest of the summer and whatever that may bring like a jewel in its palms.

* * *

A day later, everyone watches from the shoreline as the first guests fly in. I'm not used to hearing or spotting the planes, so the dockhands are far faster to find the dark pinprick on the horizon, and we stare as the Beaver grows larger and larger, the dull drone filling the air. I squint, a hand over my eyes, wondering what the plane will bring. Who is on board? Who am I about to meet? The summer is about to begin; tomorrow, we're going to be thrown full force into work. The camp is ready. The beds are ready. The food is ready. The boats are ready. So I have to be ready, too.

PANTHEON

There's nothing impressive about the staff dining room. It's a ratty area that's too small for all of us to sit in at once, so it's lucky we tend to eat in groups, depending on how early we have to wake up or how late we finish our night shifts or what time the guides come off the lake. There's one long particleboard table that's chipped along the edges and at the corners, and windows that barely let in a cross-breeze, let alone any meaningful sunlight. There's a shelf in one corner with a ragtag bunch of forks and knives, but not nearly enough spoons; a random collection of mugs from Value Village and Giant Tiger; and old plastic plates that are webbed with hairline fractures.

And then there's the wall of fame. It's the first thing my eye goes to when I enter the room: a wall covered in rows of framed photos, pictures of every group of employees from every year the lodge has been operating. Each photo has similar elements: there are young men and women standing on the shoreline, dressed in identical uniforms, staring into the camera with smiles. The pictures are lined up in order of year, with the oldest at the far left of the wall, and the most recent at the far right, and under each picture is a plaque with a list of the staff names. Despite the similarities, each picture is distinctive, based on the way these young people hold their bodies, or the angles of their heads, or the proximity they have to one another. I try to guess how each year got along by looking at their faces—if they told jokes in their time off, if they spent their afternoons alone in their bunks. It's funny to look at the staff from the eighties and nineties and see what has changed and what has remained the same. In the photos from the eighties, women are dressed in cuffed sweaters and sweatpants, their hair crimped or pulled back with scrunchies. More recent years see staff members posed awkwardly, caught mid-sentence, not used to the speed of digital photography or the harsh, flat flash. Sometimes the lake in the background rumbles with rain; sometimes it sits glazed and well behaved. I'm struck by how the facial expressions remain consistent throughout the years—there's a prevalent hope and a subtle, barefaced happiness.

I should feel reassured by these pictures, by the happiness I think I see in every small face, but I'm unsettled. I'm worried that the cohesion—a hand casually placed on the leg of the next person, an arm around another set of shoulders, two house-keepers half-turned to each other, caught in the middle of a sweet, silent joke—won't come for my year. These old photos hang over us like religious icons; they look down on us, all-knowing: *Yes, we were once like you. Yes, we turned our year into a thing of beauty, and yes, we love one another. Will you?*

When I was a guest, I sat at our family table in the dining

room and watched the white-shirted, long-necked housekeepers-cum-servers try to keep straight faces at the serving station, where they were observing us eat from out of the corners of their eyes. When I was at the dock, waiting to hop in a boat, I pulled my baseball cap low and stared at the dockhands and guides throwing lures and jerry cans and seat cushions to one another while running over rails and checking boat plugs. I was in awe of how in tune they all were, how all of the workers seemed to always be holding a smile back, as if there was always a joke following them around. As if they loved their jobs and, more important, loved the people they worked with. Therefore I, a hapless interloper, fell in love a little bit with each of them. And so, eating my eggs and watching the servers pat one another on the arms and the lower backs, their eyes soft and their bodies fluid, I made a half-thought-out choice to try my hardest to come back as a worker, to experience the other side, to immerse myself in that fierce love. But now that uneasiness that seemed to abate when we were out in the boats roars back, swirling around inside my chest. I thought we had made inroads, but this nostalgia is disorienting.

The mythology at Kesagami is rampant and important. The stories started on the train ride to Cochrane, continued at the air base bunkhouse and on the plane, and are now swapped between veterans at breakfast, lunch, and dinner. The histories of years past are told to the newbies during laundry duty or while grunting hand over hand pulling boats at the shoreline. I hear about the former dockhands, head housekeepers, and all of the staff in between. I hear about them when we clean up leaves and pick up sticks. I hear about them as we make beds and fluff pillows. I hear about them as I chew my pancakes at breakfast and stare up at their faces.

It's too early in the summer for this kind of apocrypha. It rattles me to hear about the talented, funny, strong people who came before. Maybe the veterans are feeling nostalgic for their former co-workers, are trying to suss out whether the new housekeepers and dockhands are anywhere near the calibre of former ones, but all we hear from the returnees is how previous years were so good that the reunion parties happened fast and thick, that the staff couldn't bear to be separated from one another for any amount of time. We hear that everyone is still close; we learn that they still go fishing together when they can coordinate some time off.

I stare up at the pictures of the vaunted ones with a bitter swell in my chest. We're only a week into the season, and I'm racked with doubt. What if we never get as close? What if the past hangs too heavy over all of us and we never jell? How can our year ever be so reckless, driven, fun? How can my summer ever measure up?

* * *

Housekeepers work on a seven-day rotation. We have three days of serving food—breakfast before the guests go out, dinner at night when they come in off the lake, and the occasional lunch if someone decides to stay on shore for the day—and then cleaning rooms in between the meals; one day of floater duties (doing random chores around the lodge and being present in the main building during the day in case a guest needs something); one day of bartending; one day of laundry; and one day of dishwashing. I feel completely out of place, but fast, hard days of work mean learning on the fly, so I catch up as quick as I can. I learn that there's no need to wake up so early before staff breakfast: all we need to do is roll out of bed, scrape our hair back, and stagger the short distance to the lodge's back door. I learn how to balance plates of toast and eggs on my forearms so I don't have to go back and forth to the kitchen too many times during the foggy-headed breakfast service. I learn that despite the jute, the back girls cabin still has holes in the walls, and the wind hisses through, calling to us in an unsettling way as we try to relax on our afternoons off. And I observe—very, very quickly—that the girls really do always stay on land.

Superstition holds that women aren't allowed on board working ships. Females were believed to be a distraction, bad luck. We were temptresses: sirens out of the water who would lead the sailors to ruin. At Kesagami, though, the housekeepers aren't even allowed near the water, let alone in a boat. The shoreline is for the boys, and a housekeeper who dares to break that rule is reprimanded immediately. The female staff don't ever unload the guests' luggage. We don't dock boats. We don't even get to walk on the interlock dock if there are guests present. Too close to water, too high of a chance of bad luck, maybe. There's an actual line we aren't allowed to cross on the shore, where the gravel path that leads down from the lodge ends and where the concrete of the dock base begins.

Despite what I've heard about the occasional female guest, the clientele at Kesagami seems to be mainly men, and many old-school fishermen want to see men on the lake and women in the lodge—the way it's always been, the way they always want it to be. The housekeepers kind of knew what we were getting into when we applied for this job: we knew that we were going into an old-fashioned men's world for sixty-seven days; we knew that we were going to be dealing with a male manager, a male cook, male co-workers, and mostly male guests. I'm a young woman, but even a young woman knows the full spectrum of what men can do when left to their own devices— messes made, impudence heightened, manners gone. We came into this job partly naive and partly already pushed around, as young women often are, and so now all that can be done is to buckle down, make our tips, and do what we were hired to do.

So the women do women's work. The housekeepers' chores are minutiae, little things that keep the place running without ever being perceptible, like filling the bottles of maple syrup, vacuuming the crevices of the guest rooms, replacing the toilet paper rolls, making sure the toast doesn't burn. We're made to stay inside the lodge, inside the cabins, inside the kitchen, inside the dining room; confined and passive. Meanwhile, the men do men's work. They're assigned to the forest, the open lake—dynamic places, places of motion and fresh air where they can chop and chainsaw and create and destroy. They're allowed more glory. Their work is big. They rev motors with wide arcs of their arms and dramatic grimaces, straddling the gunwales of the boats and cracking their shoulders, farting like trumpets and then laughing at themselves.

One night, I accidentally stumble upon one of these big male tasks. I've folded every last sheet and washcloth and pillowcase I could get my hands on, and now have the evening off. Instead of burrowing into my bunk like I've been doing all week, like a chickenshit trying to avoid human contact, or opting to sit on the staff beach to write letters home, I've chosen to sit at one of the picnic tables on the main shoreline. There's something about the quietness of the staff beach that frightens me; I'm not yet brave enough to sit there by myself, am too worried about what might leak out from the forest while I'm distracted. So I sit up on the higher part of the main shore, perched on a listing, splintery table, with a book in my hands but my eyes on the boys. Because, at the water's edge, those boys are beginning to congregate, filtering down from all corners of the lodge; depending on the day they've had and their personality, they stumble or sashay or stalk down to meet one another. Dockhands emerge from their cabins with a speed I've not yet seen from them; guides come in off the lake and hop out of their boats as the motor is still sputtering. The clunky, rude young men I'm slowly starting to get to know suddenly become selkies, moving together in a fierce set of dance moves in order to line up near the boat farthest from the dock.

"What are they doing?" I aim my question at Alex as she hustles past me on the waterfront path. I may have the night off, but she has to boot it to the kitchen, where she'll oversee the dinner service. Alex can be odd. I haven't spent much time with her because she spends all of her time in her bunk, writing letters to her boyfriend. She's also a complete veteran at this housekeeping business—this is her third year here, so she's already perpetrated her hijinks; she doesn't have time or patience for pranks or tit for tat. Because she can be so high-strung, I find her a little bit stressful, but mostly kind, intelligent, and good at what does. She looks out for the housekeepers in her care. She's always willing to grab a sponge, a bucket, a broom, and make sure her girls are looked after and aren't working alone. It's a quality that's rare enough in fully grown adults, never mind a twentysomething woman, and it makes her seem older than she is, in a good way.

"Pulling boats," she says, her voice trailing after her. I watch her disappear between the trees en route to the main building.

Without any obvious verbal cues, those boys line up on either side of the first freighter canoe—a few young men on each side, with the two or three left over holding the rope that's attached to the boat's prow. They grip the weight of slick gunwales; their staff shirts stick to their backs; they pull their work gloves tighter onto their hands with their teeth; they crack their lower backs and their shoulders and their necks with grim determination, practising their own form of northern shoreline yoga, preparing for the ritual. Before I can move to take a photo, or sit up straight to get a better look, Jack and Pete shout something that doesn't sound like words, and all of the men cock their heads down, bow their shoulders, and plow forward, their thighs flexing and swollen as they push the boat up the rails and into place. They bray from the stress of it, in the thick of it, moving hand over hand up the length of the coarse boat rope to heave the canoe out of the water and up onto the rails. I'm hypnotized by how beautiful it is, by its balletic danger. I'm struck, can't move, held in place by the raw, powerful movements and the way the boys immediately change from clunky, rude gawkers into dance-footed, thick-armed warriors, nimble and tight and moving entirely as one being.

As I watch them pull boat after boat, the water behind them

darkens with the slipping away of the day, and soon all I can make out are the boys' bright white teeth. I start to notice that they each have their own position, and the positions never change. Pea, Kev, Jack, and Connor hold the gunwales. Gus anchors the rope at the very end, up near the shoreline, and Aidan stands beside him. Pete brings up the rear, a coxswain, shouting that everyone should keep pulling, keep pulling harder, harder, *harder*.

Every evening, the boys will have to pull the boats up from the water onto the boat rails on shore. The weather has the tendency to turn nasty at night, and if a boat stays in the shallows, its bottom can get irreparably damaged from rocking along with the howling wind. It's a hard task, though, because these freighter canoes are about a thousand pounds each, and the boat rails sit at about a twenty-five-degree angle. This is a duty designed to test your attention and your agility and your strength, all after a day of serious work. The boat rails are treacherous when wet. The boys turn northern Wallendas on these slippery tightropes, trip the light fantastic, jumping from rail to slick rail mid-pull, moving their feet even as the rope is taut in their hands and the boat moving. If they fall, they get caught under the boat, break a leg, tear a muscle. If they fall, they hit their heads on the rocks, and the damage is untold, frightening to think about. So they don't fall.

· · ·

"Tell me the best stories from your years up here," I say to Pea. The other veterans exchange looks and smile slowly. Dinner is over, so we have some time to sit and shoot the shit. Jack adjusts the buckles on his waders as Alisa flicks at her split ends. Farther down the table, Sydney is spooning cherry pie into her mouth and talking to Robin about the toilets she cleaned today; Robin is nodding emphatically, not at all put off by hearing about bodily functions while eating. Emma is twirling a butter knife absent-mindedly in her hand, folding slices of plasticky Swiss cheese into soft slices of white bread and eating them as a kind of after-dinner snack. I'm shifting around in my chair, trying to get comfortable. *Comfortable*—I'm not at that point, not this soon, but I don't feel as awkward as I did the first few days, and so I feel brave enough to ask questions, poke around, see if I can glean any information.

"You don't know what you're getting into there, girl," Gus says from down the table, his eyes still on his plate. He's an interesting presence. He lives in the guideshack with the younger men, even though there's about a twenty-year age difference between him and the other guys in that cabin. He jokes alongside them, has the same sense of humour, but is also decidedly an adult because he has five children back in Moose Factory. Gus was one of our guides last year, on our family fishing trip, and he taught me how to cast a heavy beaver-bait lure without snagging it in the trees and laughed at me while I learned to fillet. We have a bond that's different from the other workers, but, at the same time, it's a bond that was forged when I was a paying customer. We've gone from teasing each other over cans of beer and wrangling pike lures to working on opposite sides of the rigidly enforced gender divide. I wonder how we're going to rebuild a friendship. He keeps his eyes on his chicken as he chews. I gnaw on one side of my pointer finger.

"Where do I start?" Pea rubs a hand over the lower part of his face, thinking, his eyes inscrutable below the brim of the worn green hat he never takes off.

"Well."

"*Well—*" This word is echoed, eerily and perfectly, by every veteran at the table, and I feel the hair on my arms and legs stand up at the uncanniness of it.

Jack rolls his head around on his neck, and I'm certain I hear the vertebrae click. So many people I meet are iterations of others I've known, but there's something about Jack that pulls me in immediately, treacherously. Jack is brand new. The way he speaks, the way he swears, the way he wears people down, relentless and shrill—all of these traits are alien to me, and therefore I'm drawn to him, curious and masochistic.

Jack is smart, nearly too smart for his own good: he's impertinent and impatient, says things quickly when his mouth doesn't catch up to the speed his brain is working at. His sense of humour often has the rest of the staff laughing so hard that we can only communicate through tabletop slaps and useless leg kicks. His stories and anecdotes are endless, and he knows how clever he is and that he's the natural leader. He's both the fool and the emperor, a rule-maker who will turn on you in a hot second and snitch on you to the boss if you cross him in a way he deems inappropriate, the glue that is going to keep our group together, a contradiction in all ways.

"One time I had to climb the satellite tower on top of the lodge," Jack says, green eyes unblinking.

"So?"

"Without a safety rope." He laughs. "Well, no. I had a safety rope, but it didn't attach me to the roof—it attached the power drill to my belt. Some fucking use, eh?"

"And the lodge roof is tin!" Tiff shakes her head.

"All the housekeepers were sitting in the dining room, like . . . like, fuckin' expecting to see me fall off the tower and punch through the roof into the lodge."

"I wish." This sentiment is chorused by a few of the housekeepers; it seems that Jack is interminably annoying to many.

"Why were you up there?"

"Hank wanted me to sweep cobwebs away from the satellite dish." Jack is the only one on staff who uses the pet form of Henry's name.

"Could you have said no?"

"Of course I fucking could have," Jack shoots back. I feel like there's something unspoken here: *Of course I could have, but think of the stories I'm able to tell now.*

Pea hoots a chuckle through the back of his throat. There's a beat of silence.

"Oh! What about Trevor and the dump?"

Alisa starts to shake her head, the laughter already burbling from behind her chest bones. "Oh, yeah." Her giggle, I've learned, is the most contagious in camp, a trilling, bubbling bell of a thing. So I start to laugh, marooned, without even knowing where this story is going to go.

"Yeah. One time Trevor had to do dump burn—"

"And he was so good at it, honestly," Alex says.

"He could get the fire ten, fifteen feet into the air. No one lit garbage on fire like Trev. None of these idiots our year can compare," Jack continues.

Alex nods. Aidan, at the other end of the table, is either unaware that he's being insulted or is ignoring them.

Dump burn is the stuff of heroes. At the end of every day, all garbage—especially the food scraps—needs to be set on fire in the dump. This is supposed to deter the bears and myriad other scavengers from gathering too near to the lodge. Every dockhand over the years has had a different way of burning the dump, I hear. Some studious boys in the past knew how to layer the garbage just perfectly, so that the right amounts of oxygen and gasoline were between the strata of food bits and tampons and tissues and toilet paper rolls. Good dump burns are bragged about. And there's an element of danger to the burn, because when the summer gets crackling and dry, there's a very real risk of starting a forest fire.

"So he took Tiffany back with him. Because you're not supposed to do dump burn alone. In case something happens."

"You know."

"*You know.*"

"Well, like, thank god she was there. Because he steps on a two-by-four and it has this brutal rusty nail sticking out of it."

"Like *this* long." Tiff measures with her fingers.

"And he yells and drops the bucket of gasoline, but he bends over as he does, see?" Jack can't breathe.

"And the gas splashes up into his eyes."

"So Tiff has to figure out how to work the piss-pack!" A piss-pack is an unwieldy plastic firefighting backpack that holds just shy of twenty litres of water and has a hose that has to be pumped by hand. It's a useless safety measure up here. No one on staff really knows how to work it properly, and if a forest fire ever caught up with us, it would be just that—like pissing into hellfire.

"And she's trying to figure it out—"

"—Really, no one ever teaches the housekeepers anything useful! It's not my fault," Tiff protests.

"And he's yelling *hurry, hurry* because he can't see, because there's fuckin' *gas* in his eyes!"

The table jiggles from where Pea's palms are hitting it, his body hunched over as he laughs. Alisa has her head in her hands. There's a comfortable lull, and people go back to shovelling pie into their faces. I toy with a spoonful of cherry filling until—

"One time I killed a chipmunk by dropping a Rubbermaid box on its head," Pea says.

"Oh, God." I drop my spoon and push the bowl away.

"Well, the bastard was chewing through my Rubbermaid box!" There are nods of agreement. "So I stood with my legs on either side of the doorway to my room, and when he ran through them I dropped the box on him."

"Chipmunk jam."

I recoil.

"Yeah, all right. I felt terrible. But we had a chipmunk problem that year. Real bad. What was I supposed to do?"

"Oh, speaking of chipmunks."

"Oh Jesus, don't." Jack closes his eyes and puts a hand over his face. Tiff screws up her mouth. I watch, keenly.

"That was the only night Tiff didn't sleep in Jack's bunk,"

Alex says. "I've actually never seen that before. She came back to the front girls cabin. The only night."

"Well, I'm sorry. He put a dead chipmunk down the front of his pants and pretended it was his penis. I was so angry."

"Yeah, yeah."

"He put it through his open fly like it was his pecker!"

"All right, all right, shut up."

"She's never let him forget it, either."

"I'll say."

There's another silence as Tiff and Jack relive that moment of their relationship. If Pea weren't grinning from ear to ear, I'd feel more awkward.

Alisa breaks the quiet. Through a mouthful of dessert she says, "The housekeepers had their own fun, too, eh?"

"Oh, God. There was some weird stuff we did."

"Remember when Monica stole all of Will's socks? She was a weirdo, right? Every time she did his laundry, she took a pair of his socks and hid them in her drawers. And when we asked her what the hell she was doing, she said—"

There's a chorus of "—*Every man for himself!*"

"Remember Lenna and Suze's tit-punching game?"

"Oh yeah, oh yeah! They created this game where they had to slap each other in the tits as hard as they could. Well, one tit at a time."

"Hurts more that way."

"They'd, like, sneak up on each other."

"Suze liked to get Lenna in the dining room, behind the flue. Where the guests couldn't see. That way, Lenna couldn't yell, she had to be quiet."

Lots of laughter.

"Lenna's an actress. So the summer she worked here, she served one family and used a different accent every night. Don't know if they ever noticed."

I like these stories even better than the stories about the dock-hands. These women are goddesses of housekeeping mythology, and I look to them for inspiration.

"Oh, God. Remember Ethan in the linen closet?"

"Oh, gawd. Gaaa-a-wd!"

"Henry sent him to the attic to do some repairs."

"Can't send just anybody to the attic. One wrong step and they'd fall through the ceiling! Into the motel hallway!"

"Well, the entrance to the attic is in the housekeeping closet."

"Where we have to go to get all of our supplies!"

"He *waited* up there for—God knows how long, actually."

"I forget who it was—"

"—She came in to get a vacuum and he *dropped* from the *ceiling.*" The girls start laughing so hard they can't even open their eyes, and I can't help but join in, despite not knowing who they're talking about.

"Syrup," Aidan says from farther down the table, interrupting my thoughts.

As I reach for the syrup, my fingers slip, and I knock the bottle over. Kevin is fast enough to cradle it in his palm before it hits the table and spills, and for that I'm grateful. The rest of the staff chuckles as he rights it.

"Easy, big rig," he croons, the way a man might talk to a frenzied horse.

My mouth falls open. "Big rig?"

Jack erupts, seizing on a moment. "I don't know about where you're from, Kev, but men don't usually call women *big rig*." He turns to me. "Isn't that right, Big Rig?"

I know that the more I protest this nickname, the more the boys will use it. I also don't entirely mind; part of me relishes the teasing. Again, I look at the pictures of the people above me, people who most certainly teased one another, people who probably had nicknames. Somehow, this makes me feel as if I've joined them.

*   *   *

One evening, I slip away to the shore and, without thinking, perch on the edge of the shipping platform—a lopsided wooden slab for tackle boxes and luggage, held up by empty jerry cans and old barbecue-sauce buckets, wedged at the cusp of land where the dock begins and the shore ends. I want to sit and watch the boys work, and they seem satisfied with that, because no one tells me to piss off, that women aren't allowed. Their work is fascinating, much more interesting than washing dishes or folding fitted sheets. I could sit here all night, in the funny tornado of male activity; everyone is at ease, dirty, damp from the mist that hangs heavy and sweet in the early-evening air. Without makeup on, and with my hair tucked up under a hat, I could be one of the guys, anyway; the guests don't even seem to notice a woman in their midst. And being one of the guys makes me feel better: the fear that is a constant presence, a hard little orb nestled in my torso, goes away when I can be as loud and rude as the boys.

I frown as I watch Gus rummaging around in a tackle box that doesn't seem to be his. He has a pocketknife in one hand and what looks like a guest's fishing rod in the other.

"What're you doing?"

Gus grins, not at all ashamed to be caught making mischief. "Watch," he says, snicking the knife open with a deft one-handed movement.

"That's his boat for tomorrow," Jack murmurs beside me, where he's trying to reseal a bag of black plastic twister lures. I crank around to look at Jack, but he just shakes his head, and focuses on the bait in his hands.

Gus runs his thick fingers down the fishing line, stopping right above where the lure is tied. He takes the knife and runs the blade so, so carefully back and forth across the braid.

"He's cutting it?"

Gus laughs. "Close." He's still focused on his task.

"He's *almost* cutting it," Jack says.

Gus clicks the knife closed and gently puts the rod back beside the others. He grins up at me for a second time. "Tomorrow, when they cast—"

"Oh, you shit," I inhale, and Gus laughs now, loud and clear and without malice.

"Yeppers," he says, making a casting motion with his hand, miming something flying through the air.

"Goodbye lure," Kev hollers from across the rails.

"I hope it's not their favourite," I say, shaking my head.

Gus shrugs.

"He's put rocks into shore-lunch kits before, too," Jack says, sniffing his fingers. "So the guests have trouble carrying them from the boat. This stink bait smell good?" He waggles his fingers at me, and I jerk back. The guys laugh, but it doesn't feel mean. It feels like being part of a pack.

The air gets heavier as a mild rain rolls in. I lean my head back and feel the wetness speckle across my brows and eyelids, shivering with the pleasure of it. Kevin offers me his jacket. Standing between my legs, he buttons me into it, the inner cuffs—silk, for warmth—damp around my wrists. I smile at him; he smiles back, shy, pretty, nothing but kind. I want to say *thank you, when you're nice to me I don't feel as stupid as I normally do*, but the words are lodged at the back of my mouth. I don't want to appear maudlin in front of anyone, don't need to give these boys a look into my emotions.

Henry appears on the shoreline. He's holding himself ramrod straight, and his eyes are fixed on me as he moves through the fishermen, greeting the stragglers coming off the lake. He can't yell because there are guests around. Instead, he walks up to me, smiling a pike-tooth grin, pinning me in place even as some of the boys have already skittered away.

Henry looks at me, but doesn't address me. Instead, he speaks to Kev.

"Kevin," he says. "There's a problem here. Do you know what it is?"

I shrug, answering for Kev.

"It's this *lovely* lady sitting right here. Where should she be?"

I don't answer because I don't trust myself not to snap back. Aren't I here, up here, no matter what? Why, in this swath of wilderness, would there be a place I'm not supposed to be? Shouldn't it be every woman for herself, any port in a storm?

Aren't I supposed to be here, leaning back on my hands, feeling the paint peeling beneath my palms so much that I come away with flecks in my love lines? Watching the physical work of men and wishing I could help?

Apparently, I'm not.

"You don't have to move right now," Henry finally says directly to me, as if he's doing me a favour.

When he leaves, just as quickly as he came, still glad-handing the guests, I slip out of Kevin's jacket. I'm too humiliated to offer any backchat to the boys who are watching me go. I walk away from the shoreline, back into the forest, to the girls' cabin, to my bed, to the quieter, smaller female places.

● ● ●

When it rains, the tin roof of the main building sounds like so many things at once: a solo snare in a drumline or a rollicking of heels and fists in a tantrum state or a toothy monsoon rearing up toward us. I'm getting ready for dinner service when I hear the rain start, and I can tell it's going to be a thick one, the kind of rain that rails so loudly against the walls and eaves that I won't be able to hear my guests place their orders even though I'm standing a foot away. But there's something about rain like this that makes us twitchy and thrilled. It's a vestige of childhood, the idea of a puddle day, a rain check.

Once it starts, I'm grateful most guests give only one-word answers to my rote questions: Russian or Italian dressing? Beef medium rare or medium well? Yorkshire pudding or no? Earlier in the summer is when the more dedicated fishermen tend to come up, so conversation with the guests is limited. There are moments when these crotchety men show their hands, when they grin to themselves when thinking about a successful day on the water, when they rub their fingers together while waiting for dinner, remembering the slick feel of fish scales on the skin. There's joy to be found, and even the grumpiest guests are able to get a taste of it. But the housekeepers aren't thinking about the guests at the moment. Instead, our eyes are cast on the plateau of the lake beyond the dining room windows, where the water is shifting from bronze to grey, frothing and belching along the sandy shoreline as if violent hands were tatting it, stirring it, beckoning us to watch up close.

When we finish serving dinner, some of the girls make a dash for the cabins, wanting only to step out of proper pants and into sweats and let the inescapable aggravations of the day dissolve under the rhythms on our windows and the smell of fresh water on the breeze. But some of us pull on our jackets, our shells, rain pants and bibs and waders borrowed from the main lodge, abandoned boots pilfered from the back corners of closets and adopted as our own. We don't know how long the rain will last. There's a saying up here: *Don't like the weather? Wait fifteen minutes!* We can't risk a delay.

Henry won't be outside in weather like this. He prefers the lodge, the ability to check and recheck weather systems obsessively on his satellite internet. Right now, he'll be strolling between the rows of tables in the dining room, leaning down to tell people how fierce the current "system" is, how long it'll be overhead. These pronouncements are almost always wrong, but the fishermen like being reassured. And because he's inside, we're outside. Pea, Jack, Connor, Aidan, and Kev are already sitting on the shipping platform, watching the lightning skitter across the lake, and Alex, Syd, Alisa, and I join.

No hesitation. No frittering. The line of gravel and concrete that's supposed to deter us has been muddied by the rain, anyway. The downpour is strong: it has tibiae, a diamond-ringed gullet, bear claws. It gnaws at us, already dripping down our waistbands and our collars, despite our best efforts to swathe ourselves against it. It slashes sideways, washes our faces, wets our tongues. Rinses away the hot words we felt the urge to say throughout the day. We wedge in beside the boys, ass to ass and elbow to elbow, and I smile because the platform is so high off the ground that our feet dangle.

From behind, we might all look the same—brightly coloured lumps subtly bobbing up and down on the spot as a result of our legs swinging back and forth from the height of the platform; that's how excited we are. Our hoods are cinched tight around our eyes. There are no big or little motions, no breasts or stubble that would delineate us from one another. We're hideous and bulky, strong, damp, squished body against body, instinctively huddling each time the thunder bays and barks. It's dangerous, sitting here and tracking the lightning as it vaults across the water. We're too close to the action. The sky is so rimed with clouds that we swear, later, that we could actually see the thunder. The lightning turns red across the bay—a phenomenon I've never seen—and around us, forest fires start from the top down; for the rest of the summer we will remain on smoke watch, wondering if we'll ever be engulfed.

We taste the static on the air, like cling wrap and lime juice. We smell the fish scales in the wild wind, all of the things brought up from the bottom of the lake, like old fish bones, Silver Minnow lures rusted with lust and patience. We're reduced only to our senses. What we see, smell, want. What we feel from one another's bodies. What we feel in our spines every time the sky rolls.

We're tiny. We're at our most febrile, heat folding away into the snap of the storm like egg whites into batter, the weather perched on the cusp of the sunset that is blithely proceeding somewhere unseen behind the gale. We're awake, feverish. It's arousal, though not yet for male or female, because in the face of the greatest storm we've ever seen, we can't spare a thought for that kind of longing. Instead, we howl up to the sky and grab one another's shoulders and stomachs and calves. I'm soaked to my bones, my quiet frustration leaking out of me like it's being pulled back to the place where all emotion comes from.

*　*　*

When I return to my cabin, breathless, my hair plastered to my neck and shoulders, I discover that there's a hole in the roof right above my bunk, and my mattress is damp, so Syd mixes an unused tampon with old jute pried out of the walls and shoves it in the hole, slapping some duct tape overtop. My heart swells at this action, at this clever, take-no-shit girl and her helping me, and our cabin inches closer to becoming friends.

That night, I think we'll never be able to fall asleep, but all of us close our eyes at the same time, some of us folding damp hands under pillows, and when we wake up the next morning, we've dreamt of nothing and slept without rupture. We're tall and green and loose-limbed from the depletion of electricity in the air. Our rain gear will dry, and the housekeepers will never again get to sit on the shipping platform without reproach, but it doesn't matter. Because we all yipped, swung our legs off the edge, wet our necks and mouths with rain. For that reckless moment, we were the same.

THE FLOCK

I watch as Pea makes homemade buoys out of bleach jugs. It's a quiet day on shore. Nice weather means all of the guests are out on the lake, and will stay out until it's late. On bad-weather days, a number of guests stay on dry land, and the housekeepers are expected to be friendly faces around to help. We forgo breaks and serve lunch instead of taking much-needed afternoon naps. Everyone hopes for good-weather days—the guides make money out on the water, the housekeepers get to sit and write letters home, and the dockhands get to complete the never-ending chores Henry's asked of them.

Pea's hands are dexterous as he threads a yellow nylon cord through the jug handles. We're tucked back in the clearing, a messy gap in the trees where the lodge's generator and a woodpile and the dockhand shed are kept away from the guests' eyes. Pea is one of the lodge's mysteries. Everyone keeps telling me his nickname is Sweetpea because he's so kind, so obliging, but nothing I've seen so far has confirmed this for me. In fact, he seems brusquer than most of the other male staff. I wonder if it's because I haven't proved myself—I'm always aware of my privilege, switching allegiances from guest last year to worker this year—so I try to show him that I'm willing to work hard, willing to learn, willing to listen when he's willing to impart some of the knowledge he's accrued working here over many years. *Please just be nice to me,* I want to say. *All I want to do is work hard and not be an asshole. I know I don't belong in this world. I know everyone thinks that, too.*

"You know they're scavengers, right?" His voice is quiet, distracted.

"Huh?"

"The eagles," Pea says, knotting the cord and throwing the new buoy onto the ground.

He's referring to the last boat of the morning, full of Texans, who had jetted across the lake in a babble about finding eagle feathers. It's a given that guests are particularly enamoured with the eagles, both bald and golden; the men love to come in off the lake and tell me stories about these birds, which I don't get to see. For the most part, the eagles stay far away from the shore. They have little use for loud, rude humans, and spend their days mainly on the lake, hunting for fish, the primary staple of their diet. Because the dockhands and housekeepers are just focused on staying upright on a daily basis, we don't think much about the eagles. They don't bother us; we don't bother them.

"They follow the boats and try to steal the fish off of guests' lines."

I stare at him for a moment, and start to laugh.

"What?" He can't figure out if I'm laughing at him, or if I'm starting to lose it. But I can't help it. The idea of fearsome predators stooping to scavenge—that the image I had of the eagle is completely different from reality, that my romantic notions about the North are probably mostly wrong—is so very like the lodge. Because in this place, all energy goes toward staying alive. All avenues are acceptable.

"Never mind," I say. It would be too much to explain my thought process. "Do you need help carrying these?" I gesture to the buoys, and Pea nods, smiling a little, and piles some into my arms.

The scavenging notwithstanding, the image of bald eagles waiting in the treetops for an unassuming fisherman to tootle by in his boat, with fat fish ripe for the taking, there's something about those birds. There's a reason they're so vaunted, why they evoke such a visceral reaction in so many people, why the guests do circles in their boats, hoping for a dropped feather they can take home as a keepsake. Despite their opportunistic nature (or perhaps even because of it), the eagles are intimidating, enigmatic. They are sentinels. The guests tell me that on a quiet day on the lake, you can actually hear the deep *ka-thwip ka-thwip* of their wings when they fly close to the canoes. These giant birds represent a world we do not belong to, a world we know we're only visitors in.

You only have to look at the many forms of divination that are related to birds to see what effect they've had on humans throughout the ages: augury, the general fortune-telling that comes from observing the flights of birds; ornithoscopy and ornithomancy, the study of omens associated with birds; alectryomancy, the form of divination where someone observes a bird pecking at grain on the ground; oomancy and ovomancy, where eggs are interpreted. From eagles to waxwings to cormorants, mergansers to whiskey jacks, we have all sorts of omens above us at Kesagami: though we mostly ignore them, focused as we are on tasks on the ground, the birds could very well be some kind of magic.

I've been up close and personal with a bald eagle before. Once, in Vancouver, as my mother and I were walking down the stairs to Wreck Beach on a bleak fall day, a huge rustle of feathers made us both snap our faces up at the same time. We stopped, frozen; a bald eagle, with a fish in its talons, had flown above us, across the path, and was sitting in a tree, ready to eat. I had just moved to the city, so we thought it was a sign, some portent of how good life in Vancouver was going to be. Little did I know that it was probably the hapless fish that was the message. I didn't know what was ahead, that I would have to work harder than I had ever before, that I was going to have to learn to slog through depression and darkness so thick and webbed that, on some days, waking up would feel like tearing through a membrane, like a chick gnawing its way out of an egg, just to function at a basic level. But in that moment, the eagle felt like a guardian—or, at the very least, a sign that this odd, slick city, so obsessed with its own image and building itself up, hadn't destroyed all of the things it was actually built on. It was reassuring that the eagles and the people could somehow coexist.

●　●　●

"See that?"

I follow Alisa's finger. Farther away, over the tops of the pines, a big old crow is circling. As we drift down the shoreline,

I imagine that he's following us, too, keeping an eye on us like we're keeping an eye on him.

I make a sound of assent. Alisa paddles lazily, leaned back into the canoe seat. Somehow, we've managed to get the boat backward. Despite sitting at what I thought was the front, I'm paddling the rear. It means she has more room, and she spreads out, closes her eyes to the sun and absorbs it like a cat.

"A crow means that there's a bear nearby." Her eyes are still closed.

"How?"

"They're so smart they follow the black bears. Bears find garbage, I guess. So the crows follow and eat when the bears aren't looking."

"What?"

"Yeah, I'm not kidding," she says with a smile. "It's insane how smart they are."

Toronto has some crows, but Vancouver has flocks of them, murders of them. That was the main thing that struck me on moving to the West Coast: the crows, on every mailbox, every telephone pole, every street corner. They're everywhere, cheeky and bobbling and mouthy. My apartment window looks out at the building's fire escape; if I lean a little farther than I should, I can touch the rusted metal railing. I started putting cubes of cheese there, to see if the crows that I heard in the nearby trees in the mornings would notice, deign to come near.

It surprised me that it took a few months for them to get completely comfortable with me. From the brash braying, I assumed that crows would be fearless little fuckers, but in reality they were slow to warm, skittish. I'd put food out—cut-up cherries, pieces of cheddar, bits of popcorn—and sit at my desk with my windows open, to see if they'd land and watch me as I was watching them. At first they'd swoop down, pick up the treats, and fly off as fast as they could. But as the weeks passed, they would sit and stare back. Eventually, all I had to do was open my windows and they would hover down and keep me company. And I looked forward to it, because I was lonely. Because writing is lonesome and dire, no matter how amazing it feels in the end. Writers are incredibly lucky: we're a privileged bunch, to be paid to do what we love, but we also hate what we do because we're alone. I liked being alone, but loneliness was a different story. And when I had the birds on my fire escape, I didn't feel that lonely.

At Kesagami, the corvids (the smart family of birds that includes crows, ravens, and grey jays, among others) are mostly blaring bullies, so like my crows at home in their fierce and skittish nature, and yet so unlike them at the same time. Kesagami crows caw at full volume in between rolling clicks and grunts. They're rude and pushy and loud, which makes them my favourites. Of all the birds we see, the crows are the most similar to our own cabal of squawking, squealing young people, loud and lusty and willing to shout to get a point across, yet cunning and quiet when need be.

The forest is never quiet when the corvids are talking in couplets, and the rich mythology that surrounds this family of birds is neither easy nor straightforward. Throughout history, and across the world, the raven (and, often, the crow by association, since they look and act so similar) has been portrayed as many things, from a trickster to a creator god, a warrior to a harbinger of death and doom. In ancient Greece, ravens were associated with Apollo, god of prophecy, and were considered good luck. In Viking mythology, the ravens Hugin (thought) and Munin (memory) were Odin's eyes and ears, bringing the god news from around the world. In Irish lore, the crow is associated with the Morrigan, the "phantom queen" of war and sovereignty. Morrigan and her sisters, Macha and Badb, became a trio of battle goddesses known as the great queens. In the far east of Russia, the Koryak people worship the shamanistic trickster and fertility figure of Big Raven, who is also known as Quikil, Kutkh, or Kytx. At the Tower of London, at least six ravens are kept on the grounds at all times; legend says that if the ravens ever leave, the Tower and the kingdom will fall. All this mythology lends to the corvids' complicated status as birdbrain and genius, a benevolent god and a chaotic prankster, good and evil.

*   *   *

Alisa dips her paddle and splashes me a little, startling me, and I laugh. She grins back, shading her face with one small hand. The two of us sit there, smiling like idiots. I've started to really enjoy her company. There's something incredibly pure about her, which is a difficult quality to maintain up here. If something bad happens, Alisa sheds it with her perfect, bell-like giggle, and the rest of us can't help but also laugh. She's full of a joy that is rarely diminished, and she takes the shitty things alongside the good things with a shrug. Since we served breakfast together this morning, I'm lucky to have an afternoon off with her.

Suddenly, there's a holler. Tiff and Alex motion to us from shore, where they've been sitting under a tree reading old issues of *Cosmo* and *Seventeen*. Jack stands behind them, his face obscured by the tree's shadow. All three of them watch as I prod Alisa with a paddle.

She twists in her seat. "Oh, they want us to bring the canoe in."

As we get closer to shore, Jack steps out of the shade and starts to undo his jeans. This is, surprisingly, a common occurrence; I think he's going to moon us. When he takes off his shoes, I sit up straighter. Alisa, facing me and coming into shore backward, can't see what's happening on the beach, but she can see my face. My eyes bug as Jack whips his hat off. When he starts sprinting, I scream at the top of my lungs. Alisa thrashes and cranes her head as Jack blasts toward us at full speed, his knees raised as he high-steps across the rocks and silt, the water spraying like wings. The two of us paddle away as hard as we can, but Jack reaches the canoe before we can escape. He grabs our flailing wrists and yanks simultaneously on our bodies and the lip of the boat, sending us ass over teakettle into the shallows, our legs straight up in the air, his trickster laughter blaring inside the husk of the canoe. On shore, the girls laugh. The crows laugh. Underwater, even we laugh. When we come up, our hair streams around our faces and feathers down our backs.

• • •

Not even a few weeks into the summer and I miss both of my cities. It's an odd thing, splitting your heart between two places.

Because it's where I grew up, I think about Toronto the most; it's the place I feel most comfortable, even if I don't always feel totally comfortable there. Toronto is hard and wry; it's unforgiving and fast and contains flashes of beauty in between its expanses of grey—its colourless slush, its chipped curbs, its mottled subway cars and dusty buses. But if you're adept, you can find enough of Toronto's glowing jewels to keep yourself fed for the rest of your life, because the city never stops moving, growing, changing, and it drags all of its inhabitants along with it, never letting us become complacent or have time to rest and replenish.

If Toronto is relentless and has a streak of meanness, Vancouver is softer and seems, to the outsider's eye, all-over beautiful. I'm still an outsider in Vancouver, and might be forever, even if I lived the rest of my life there, which I already know won't happen. Vancouver's beauty is completely unfolded, spread out luxuriously for the eye as soon as you step off the plane, the SkyTrain, out of your apartment into the constant, heavy fabric of rain. But Vancouver has jags of hideousness hidden in between the folds of its allure. It has a smile that's wide and white-toothed, but in the back of its mouth there's decay. Vancouver isn't mad like Toronto: it's sad, sagging at the seams, carrying a giant, damp yoke. And Vancouver keeps me on edge in a way Toronto never has: I'm disconcerted that people who live there rarely seem to acknowledge its most serious problems. Still, there are things about living there that I love—strong drinks on gay-bingo nights, trees on the university campus, long nights of pints with the writers I love, classmates who are sharp and kind and talented and who cheer me on in my writing as much as I try to cheer them on in their own.

The cities beckon, even now. But if I were back in the city, working some familiar, mindless job and ensconced in a metal haze, in the dust-tasting and sludge-smelling grid of metropolis, I wouldn't be able to do this: sit on the shore on my nights off and see things. The impending gloaming purpling its way to camp, pleating in from the tops of the trees and the lake's horizon. The private smiles of fishermen who stagger out of the boats after a long day on the water and hundreds of fish caught. The tense sensuality of boat pull. The boys dipping their heads, joking and waiting for the last guests to come in for the night. The boys cuffing one another on the shoulders and the backs of heads, murmuring about the girls, flicking one another's body parts. The boys calling geese.

In the city—any city—Canada geese annoy the hell out of me. They are evil, malicious, and violent, and I wonder why we don't actively get rid of them. They gather in baleful flocks, terrorizing people, slicking the ground putrid green with their shit. Up here, though, they're different: gun-shy, feral, less complacent. Sweeter. Odder. They're too wary to land near us, and rarely fly close; they exist to me only as a V across the setting-sun sky, an echoing chorus of honks, something that reminds me of home without seeming like home at all.

The geese fly at unexpected times. The dockhands might be pulling boats or chopping wood, and the honk will start from one edge of the lake, so soft I don't even hear it at first, but not soft enough to escape ears more attuned than mine. That's when the guides' heads pop up from behind the boat rails, one at a time, and the boys amble down from the high shore to the edge of the water. Their sun-browned faces soften with pleasure as they turn to the sky. Their eyes close in preparation for a moment of showing off.

The fishing guides and dockhands can call flying geese out of flock formation. I don't know how they do it, what unseen efforts lead to the jarring two-tone echo of the goose cry. Maybe it's in the contraction of the glottis, the squeeze and release of the sleekest muscles of the throat. Maybe it's in the angle of their heads. Maybe it's magic. Most likely, it's an out-of-city thing. There are wooden calls designed for this—Kevin has a string of them hanging from his bunk bed—but there's more pride in being able to lure a flock with just natural aptitude. Many of the guys hunt, know how to field dress a deer, how to fillet a fish on a board on a bucket in the middle of a moving boat. They know how to stalk bears, how to start even the crankiest Husqvarna chainsaw. A good number of the lodge employees, including some of the women, all attend the same outdoor college. They're aiming toward degrees in fish and wildlife, arboriculture, aquaculture, outdoor adventure skills. My in-progress writing degree falls flat in comparison.

"What are you taking in school, Anna?" Jack asks me one night at dinner, a smile on his shit-eating face. He already knows—everyone knows everyone's business—but he wants to start a conversation and so he's prodding.

"Writing," I start. I don't get to finish, because the rest of the guys erupt. They lean back and hoot and blare.

"Arts degree! Arts and crafts," Jack says. "What do you do in arts and crafts, Anna?"

"I bet you make paper-plate tambourines!"

"Do you put rice in your tambourines, Anna?"

"Dried beans?"

"Peas?"

"Is that how you get your degree? Show them your tambourine? Do you know how to play tambourine?"

They must have planned this; the responses are too choreographed to be something random. I don't tell them what I want to say—*You fucking idiots. I can write. I'm good at something too.* Instead, I lift my shoulders, try not to show weakness. "Yeah," I say. "Master of fine arts. MFA. Stands for master of fuck all."

This earns me a laugh, which makes me feel a bit better. The moment is broken up as Henry pokes his head into the room with a frown on his face.

"If you get any louder, the guests at the bar are going to be able to hear you."

Some of the girls roll their eyes, trying to keep it hidden under the brims of hats or the edges of hoods. Some of the guys pick their teeth with the tines of their forks, purposefully avoiding his gaze. We think we're being subtle in our small acts of disobedience, but Henry has the knack of knowing all.

"Okay, okay," Kev says around a mouthful of pizza.

"And you have five minutes to finish up before I need the housekeepers to get ready to go out into the dining room," Henry says to everyone wearing serving whites before he slips around the jamb and disappears.

● ● ●

Connor leans over.

"It's easy to do, gal," he says.

Kevin rolls his eyes. "As if."

Connor is trying to teach me to call geese. He shakes his head at Kev, silently chiding him, and turns to me.

"You just have to say *luke*."

"Pardon?"

"*Luke, luke, luke*. Just say it over and over, real fast. *Luke*. You'll call 'em."

The three of us are sitting at the staff picnic table: Kev has a day off from the lake, and Connor has finished his chores, and so I've asked them about calling.

"I can't do that!" It's not so much that I can't do it; maybe I could, if I tried. But I can't bring myself to actually open my mouth and say the words; I feel myself blushing. It mortifies me in the same way that singing in public does. It's performance in front of people who know what they're doing, and I decidedly do not know what I'm doing. I whisper *luke* under my breath, and Kev giggles. Connor hides a smile. *Luke*. Lukewarm. I don't think there'll be any geese filtering my way.

But it can't just be that, repeating one word over and over again. Hollering *luke* at the top of your lungs is all well and good, but even Connor's missing something—the throat jump, the muscle contraction that leads to the deeper, harsher sound. I know that some of the other men can call like that. When I hear them, it makes the hair on my arms and legs stand up. The first time I heard it, I dropped my rake and stood, frozen, cocking my ears, craning my neck and looking up for the geese that didn't exist.

I know I won't be able to do it. I know I'll probably never feel completely comfortable in this place. At the same time, I'm enamoured with the sweet kind of loneliness I've uncovered in Northern Ontario. I always knew that there was a deeper significance to uncover about this land—that somewhere north, the petticoats of the country unfolded themselves to reveal an underbelly hard and old and unforgiving. I always knew that there was a sky bigger than the one pinned up, lackadaisically, over the Big Smoke.

I don't know if I'll be able to go back to the city and feel at home. Maybe my experience in the North will change me indelibly. It seems like such a frivolous thing to worry about: city slicker anxious that concrete and asphalt won't feel familiar under her heels, that the forest will gnaw out the part of her that makes a metropolis feel like home. But even now, even here, there's something about Toronto—its listless streetcars, the vast parks cradling couples, its stinking and seductive maw—that calls me out of place. There's something about Vancouver—its rich, dark mountains, its lacy mist of rain, its desperation— that makes me question formation, the idea of belonging. I'm existing between two concepts of myself, the city and not-the-city, and I can't figure out where I'm supposed to land.

Up here, where the world has started to offer itself to my imagination in every regard, I'm able to find something poignant in the honk of the geese. I like to think that they're watching us, wondering who the silly mammals are down below, wondering why we don't move in the V-formation, too.

Maybe I don't need to learn to call geese. Truth be told, I'm fine with never learning that skill—it's not in my wheelhouse, and these aren't my talents. Instead, I sit back and watch as Jack, Gus, Kev, and Connor crouch close to the ground and flick their heads back when they see a flock spackled against the sky. The guys cast silhouettes against the strange, burnished glow of the setting sun. They're not quite in that V-formation, but they stretch, walk, laugh together as a group, loud and in line and comfortable with one another. For all their rudeness, those boys are never as wild as when they gather together on bent knees like this. This is their strength, and it makes me fall in love with them even a little bit more.

How is it that the sounds that I found so irritating in the city have carved out a new place in my heart? How is it that I thought geese were ugly and malevolent? This is our link, this ornithomancy. The sky ribbons through both the city and the forest, connects the view from a fire escape with the view from a lonesome dock. If I look hard enough, long enough, there are messages to be seen from on high. An eagle perched on a branch means that even the noblest have to unbend to survive. A crow on a fire escape means laughter is near, means you're about to get taken down a few notches. A goose in the sky means that despite loneliness being wild and harsh around your heart, despite the fact that you feel forlorn sometimes when the bowl of the firmament seems too vast for you to mean anything, there's a place for you, and you'll find it.

CAKE

"Cake time, boys!"

Pea's announcement at the breakfast table confuses me because the veteran men groan and the veteran women snicker while the new staff just look bewildered.

I lean over to Alisa, trying to talk as quietly as possible. "Like, Sam's baking—"

She shakes her head violently. "No. No."

Jack hears our exchange and laughs like a horn. "You wanna know what cake is, Big Rig? Meet us at the septic tank this afternoon."

I stop buttering my bread and take the slice of cheese from between my teeth, where I was keeping it away from greedy male hands before I added it to my sandwich. Anything is up for grabs, so you have to play defence—always. "You're fucking kidding me, right?" I'm still not sure what cake is, but if it has to do with the septic tank, it's decidedly, one hundred per cent, definitely completely not something that Sam is baking, and it's also not anything remotely good, either.

Jack raises his eyebrows, still smiling.

"What—"

I don't get far into my question before Kev hollers at me from other end of the table. "Poop!"

"Obviously it's related to that if it's about the septic tank, Rook," I grumble around a mouthful of bread and cheese, using the nickname he hates so much in an attempt to deflect attention.

Jack, Pea, Alex, and Tiff guffaw, and Kev gives me the finger with a grimace. I wince a wordless apology at him, and hope he understands.

Alex takes pity on me. "It's when they empty out the septic tank using a shovel and a wheelbarrow."

Syd cocks her head. "Excuse me?"

"Not, like, every week," Alisa says.

"Yeah, more like every month," Tiff adds from a few chairs over.

"Just wait until they play the game," Alisa continues, grinning.

"Don't tell me, don't tell me, don't—"

"Tampon or fungus."

"*What!*"

"I guess there's a fungus that grows in the tank that looks a lot like tampon strings."

There are groans and hollers from both sides of the table as Henry rounds the corner, leaving his office to shush us and tell us that we have to start getting ready for the day.

"Hey batter, batter," Pete hums under his breath as we stand up to exit the staff dining room, and the boys erupt as we snake out into the main building, and I can't help but smile, too.

* * *

I never thought I'd work a job that was dictated by human shit.
It didn't even occur to me that working up close and personal
with shit would be a part of the job. Before this summer, I'd
never immersed myself in any kind of work that revolved
around the ins and outs of the human body, never had to create
a schedule or chores around human refuse. I'd worked a secre-
tarial job at a hospital; been a pro-shop employee at a snooty golf
course; helped out with arrangements in a flower store; worked
as a shop assistant at a bath-bomb chain in Vancouver. But
things change when you're following men around and cleaning
up after them. At best, it's funny and humbling. At worst, it's so
humiliating there are times when I want to cry tears of rage. The
housekeepers are not only modern-day chambermaids, we're
also plumbers, cleaning ladies, mother figures, mock-wives,
servants, and, on the bad days, whipping girls.

But mainly, we're the Queens of the Clean. Every day, after
we serve the guests their heavy, rich breakfasts of sticky eggs
and oily flapjacks, the fishermen head out on the water and the
girls run to start tidying the rooms. We start in the motel and
eventually move to the cabins, making the beds, vacuuming or
sweeping the floors, refilling the toilet paper and restocking the
tissue boxes, refolding towels that the guests left for another
day and replacing towels that need desperately to be changed.
We pick up garbage off the floor, scoop hairs out of the shower
drains and the sinks. We bend, straighten, bend, straighten, turn
messy male hovels into livable rooms all on four or five hours of
crappy sleep. We do this with aplomb and a liquid efficiency,

murmuring to one another in a housekeeper language that we all understand: linens are passed hand over hand before we fully say that we need them, glass cleaner is sprayed and the next set of hands has a wad of paper towel at the ready before the liquid has time to run down the mirror. We're masterful at what we do, and we're getting better every day.

Despite our burgeoning mastery, when it's time to clean the toilets, we always find ourselves staring down at the bowl and sighing. A weeklong trip filled with deep-fried shore lunches does funny things to a man. I predict that cleaning shit-covered toilets for a summer will do funny things to a girl, too.

The young women are always up close and personal with corporeal maleness, men's bodies. The male staff only have to deal with the toilets, with filth, if a bad clog has gotten worse and none of the girls has the arm strength or the energy to manipulate the plunger. The women deal with the guests' bodily functions on an intimate level: shit stains on the laundry, handed off without eye contact or even a mumbled "thank you," misplaced pieces of used toilet paper, and the shit that finds its way onto and *into* things we never dreamed of before coming up here.

* * *

The majority of the guests go to relieve themselves in the bathhouse since there's no running water in the cabins and walking to the motel for the nicer flush toilets takes too long. The housekeepers say a little prayer before entering the bathhouse despite there being only two toilets to deal with.

One is in a little wooden stall: a large man can't fit in there and shut the door, so the toilet often stays unused and we don't wince when we look in. But the second toilet is tucked back into a dark corner, in a much bigger stall that has its own window and a large supply of toilet paper. Comparatively, it's a bathroom fit for a king, if said king is apt to take a shit on the floor of his castle. The unlucky housekeeper on bathroom duty that day gently swings the door open, knowing there'll be something bad in there. It's a feces lottery, and all of us cross our damn fingers that our bathhouse day won't be so bad that we have to snap our hands into the cheap latex gloves Henry provides.

But it's always bad. Sometimes, there's a thick rime of shit crawling up the toilet seat and lid like perverse lichen, spreading from the bowl with vicious tendrils. Sometimes, the men have missed the toilet completely—on purpose or by accident, who the hell knows—and have left their shit-smeared wads of toilet paper on the floor behind the bowl.

On one of my bathhouse-cleaning days, there's a piece of poop stuck to the wall like a little projectile, as if one of the guests pulled his pants down, bent over, aimed, and let rip. I stand and stare for a moment before yelling a wordless invocation at the top of my lungs. My witchery works, because some of the other housekeepers come running from the cabins where they were making beds, thinking that maybe I found a particularly gnarly bug or that the dockhands have pinched my basket of cleaning supplies and run away with it, a common prank. When Aubrey, Tiff, and Alisa all screech into the bathhouse, skidding across the mat on their heels like a bunch of cartoon characters, they find me standing in the darkest corner of the larger stall, and they know what's happened.

We crouch down to stare, like prospectors finding gold. At least I'm not alone for this.

"What the hell—"

"I'm more curious to know how this . . . the, you know, the physics of it," Aubrey says, cocking her head to one side as she assesses the situation.

I nod. We stare some more. I can feel Alisa jiggling beside me, and I already know she's laughing the kind of hard, quiet laugh that's too strong to control. Tiff has her hand over her brow, looking up at the shit on the wall from between her rigid fingers, basically speechless. "Did he—did he aim?"

"Either that, or he did it with his hands," Alisa says in a choked voice, and that's when we all dissolve, hunched in the shadowy corner, bent at the waist, arms wrapped around one another as we laugh and laugh and laugh. If we don't laugh, we might cry at the idea of cleaning a man's excrement off a wall because that's our job.

The mess never ceases to amaze me. From ripped-apart beds to clothes thrown across cabin floors to explosive shit in the toilet bowls, it boggles the mind. Why does getting away from home become synonymous with guests losing their sense of propriety? It's as if the angry part of the wilderness—the part that turns people into predators—leaches into every male psyche, turns every guest into some primeval version of himself. Too lazy to throw the toilet paper directly into the toilet? No problem—chuck it on the floor for a girl to pick up. Too drunk to aim properly into the urinal? Piss on the floor and wait for the housekeepers to come and clean it. Left your pubic hairs all over the bedsheets? The girls will wash it. The girls will. The girls will. The girls always will, on hands and knees, eyes to the floor.

* * *

It's a quieter night in the lodge, with only two thirtysomething men at the bar. They're both Americans, dressed in camo sweaters, and fairly well behaved in that they're not getting shit-faced or making lewd comments, so I'm acting along and being as patient as I can be, in between moments of covertly watching the clock.

"You know, youse guys are different," one of them says.

My bartending shift is my least favourite shift. When a housekeeper tends the bar, she has to stay alone in the lodge until the last guest leaves. Although Henry sleeps in the main building, and technically his bedroom is right behind the bar wall—"Bang on the wall if you get into trouble and need someone to intervene," I'm told by Tiff and Alex when they explain how the bar shift works—it's unnerving to fend for yourself with only fishermen to keep you company. Most of the guests behave themselves. The majority don't drink that much, because there's nothing worse than waking up early with a hangover and then spending an entire day in a boat on choppy water. But there are a few outliers, and times when I feel genuinely unsettled. There was a tall, thin-haired guy who apparently scouts for an NHL farm team, who asked me if my nickname is "Big Rig" because I have a big ass; he was the last one to leave the bar that night, after having stayed far too long, and as soon as the door shut behind him, I ran to lock it.

If I were dating someone on staff, this is where they'd most come in handy. Male partners of housekeepers are known to hang around the lodge, covert and hoping Henry doesn't walk in and see them, to wait for their girlfriend to finish her shift, just to be able to walk her back to her cabin. Whether this is to provide protection from the guests or the bears—or both— I'm not sure. But I don't have a boyfriend, so aside from the odd housekeeper who filters through the lodge to say goodnight on her way to her bunk, it's me and the guests.

Tonight isn't so bad. The two of them are drinking red eyes, made of tomato juice and beer and steak sauce, and chatting about their catches of the day.

"What's different?" I crack open another Coors Light to mix a drink.

Sometimes, when I least expect it, the guests come up with real gems: existential, philosophical, spiritual jags of genius that tumble out of them at inopportune times. Maybe this will be one of those moments.

"You Canucks say 'shit' a whole lot."

Maybe not.

His words stay with me, though, and I start to notice that when Canadian guests fill the camp, the air is an orchestra of the word in its different forms. And *shit* is such a good word to say when frustrated. If people hail from smaller towns, they drag it out into two syllables, even three if they're especially talented. The word starts out susurrant and deceptive, and then ends in a plosive punch. *Shee-iit.* Of course, the female workers can't swear around the guests. But the dockhands and guides use the word liberally, because when they do, it's hilarious somehow. Our best guides are the filthiest, as if their swearing ability is as important as the calluses on their middle fingers from feeling the tension of the fishing line. Testing the way the lures dance and scrape over the rubble at the bottom of the lake through the pads of their fingers. *Shee-iit.*

Being one of the new girls, I didn't want to turn anyone off, so I tamped down my natural inclination to let a swear word rip, ripe and perfect, when I most needed to. I didn't want Henry or, even worse, a guest to overhear me spewing rudeness in a moment of frustration, and there were so many moments of frustration in the first days. Moments of feeling trapped or stupid or angry with my lot for the summer. But now, as my body starts to learn to function without my brain always guiding it, forging my new muscle memory, and as I learn to joke at the expense of myself alongside the other idiots I work with, I can feel it swelling at the base of my tongue and in the back of my throat. The shit lexicon. The filth vocabulary. The need to let loose like a snapped line, to throw my head back and howl *shee-iit* at the kitchen sink, at the unfolded laundry, at the dirty toilets, and feel my tension slide away.

All of us seem to feel it. The shift is slow and insidious—a rude word whispered alone in a guest room here, a bathroom joke that flits through our minds at the breakfast table there— but it's present now after so many damn days of trying to be polite and upstanding people. Maybe it was the shit on the wall that broke the girls. Maybe it was the thought of cake that upended the boys. Or maybe we were always just dirty-mouthed shitheads. So it lingers, hidden, waiting for the right time to fly out of us and make its point, take over our vocabulary until we can't quite recognize our old selves.

                •   •   •

Robin comes running out of the staff bathroom, her braids flying behind her. Syd and I stare as she barrels toward us.

"What, man, what?"

"I clogged the staff toilet!"

"Your shit was that large?" I ask.

Robin punches me in the shoulder as Syd starts laughing. "No," Robin says, "I accidentally flushed the wooden toilet paper roll!"

"Aw, *shee-it.*"

Our lives revolve around that toilet. It's the only toilet in camp that's reserved for staff members, that the guests don't get to sully. The housekeepers go in shifts, sprinting to the bathroom in the morning to try to get first dibs. We're in trouble.

Syd, Robin, and I run to the shoreline where the dockhands are working, and we holler one-syllable names on our way down the path—*Jack, Pea, Jack, Pea!* The two of them are inspecting the boat motors.

Jack rolls his eyes. "What did you idiots do?"

His solution is to drain the toilet, take it off of its pipes, and lug it out onto the lawn to examine it. It's a two-person job at most, but the five of us crowd around our little porcelain demigod. It's funny to see the thing that our lives revolve around removed from its natural habitat.

Pea produces a wire hanger, pilfered from a guest room. He bends it and scrapes the dried shit out of the bowl and off the pipes, rolling his eyes in an effort to look blasé, and trying not to laugh. He might be fed up with us, but he's also not outwardly chiding us. I appreciate that, in this moment. While Pea's working on the inside of the bowl, Syd's busy getting in his way as she tries to clean the outside of the bowl using Vim and a handful of paper towel, knowing that the task is insurmountable but trying anyway. Jack goes to extricate the roll from the pipe in the floor of the bathroom, swearing under his breath. The rest of us are doubled over, unable to breathe from how funny we're finding this entire situation. It's an absurd combination—Pea cranking a mangled hanger, Syd yelping as she tries to scrub years-old scum. When we reattach the thing and it works again, we all cheer.

That night, to make Robin feel better—she's been given the nickname "Flush"—Jack tells a story over dinner that ends with a moral I'll never forget. *Never use lily pads to wipe your ass.* Apparently, they're too slippery. He tells us that he found this out the hard way, the same way he discovered that you should always bring napkins with you on a winter hunting trip, especially if you've hiked away from main camp. Especially if you're alone in the middle of the snow, admiring the gleam of it, and an upset stomach strikes. And especially if you're wearing skin-tight long johns meant to keep you as warm as possible.

"Wait, what? Why? What's the issue?"

"The shit bubbles up over the waistband of the long johns, Big Rig! Upset stomach! Jesus. Use your goddamn imagination, you're a fucking writer after all."

Someone interjects with a different piece of advice: *You're not a man until you've shit your pants twice and had poison ivy on your ballsack.* Having never heard that particular maxim before, I start laughing so hard that I put my head on the table. We're all laughing. The earlier mania of our plumbing chore has transferred to the now. A few of the girls are still serving supper, but with the sunset imminent and the guests finally leaving the dining room, more and more of us filter into the staff dining room, spoons of leftover fruit crisp in our hands, faces lit up with the late light, with the sweet ease of true comfort. We have some happiness from the knowledge that for today, the dirty work is done.

⁂

I still don't know what happens if the septic tank isn't emptied. Do the wooden doors that cover the tanks explode in a geyser of human waste? It's not made clear, but we know that nothing good will come of letting it fill up. This means two boys have to pull on their hardiest rubber boots and get the shit-barrow—the wheelbarrow designated only for cake, though I don't see any specific markings on it that would tell me that—and some shovels. They have to unlatch the tank door and scoop the fermented shit out, shovelful by shovelful, and dump it into the barrow, which is then emptied in a secret spot in the woods. It turns out you either have a cake stomach or you don't, and all of the veteran male workers make a game of seeing who of the new dockhands will run into the dense weft of the forest to puke their guts out.

I don't know why I'm surprised by the disgusting nature of this particular task. Every chore is done differently from the way it might be performed in the city. Every task becomes a little more twisted. When the housekeepers are told to wash the exteriors of all of the old guest Thermoses, we don't just have to wash them, we have to use pure paint thinner to try to scrub the tape glue off of them. When a dockhand is told to sit at the wood splitter and make kindling, he doesn't just do it for an hour, he does it for an entire day, building an igloo of logs around him. By evening, we can't even see him for the wall of wood. Everything here is warped to where it's just beyond recognition of what it would be like back home. Everything is a little crazier.

Human shit takes on an odd consistency when it's been sitting in a tank for days. The boys tie kerchiefs around their mouths and put earplugs up their nostrils to stop gagging, but sometimes they still, in fact, do. They make brave faces, especially when the housekeepers line up to watch them, as we stand back at a safe distance and gawk out of macabre fascination. The guys make a point of counting how many tampons have been flushed, and then berate the housekeepers for being so careless.

I don't know why it's called cake. From where I'm standing, what they're dealing with is not even remotely solid enough to resemble a baked good, and—I hate myself for making this observation, hate myself so much—it also isn't the right consistency for batter because it's not smooth enough. But the name makes perfect sense in that it doesn't make sense. It's an irreverent title for a task that fits in so well with the dire humanity of where we are. The unabashed unpretentiousness that we have all been reduced to, learning to clear away other people's by-products.

When the dockhands and guides and housekeepers sit together for lunch, we hear how the rookies measured up in the face of cake. We high-five and shove pizza slices into our mouths with bleached hands—from cleaning toilet bowls, from disinfecting the shit-barrow—as we hear about the tampon count: better than some years, not as good as others. And nobody is teased for having to shovel shit. Instead, our young men are lauded like heroes. Clapped on the shoulders and backs for their bravery. Now they have their war stories. They, too, can join in and have two new rules to live by: never use a lily pad to wipe, and if you don't get poop on your knuckles while shovelling shit out of a septic tank, you're not doing it right. And never discount shit, because it's entirely possible to find the most brilliant slices of glee in the midst of it.

When we laugh about shit, we know there's something beyond the mess. We've started to shuck our old selves. We've left our airs on the shoreline like shadfly moult; on the winding path to the lodge dump; in the barely perceptible space between the girls' bunks, all of our breathing syncing up like our periods will, all of us drawing one another in and out in the thickest parts of the night.

And once I've started to shed posture and cleanliness—once I start to learn to fold into another person without any self-consciousness, to laugh, open-bellied and with tears on my face, about shit, or *shee-it*, in all of its forms, liquids and solids, stains and accidents and smears and projectiles—there's nothing that keeps me from being the richest version of myself I can be.

NO-WOMAN'S LAND

"Horseflies always fly to the highest point on a body, you know."

I'm washing the outside of the lodge windows, up on a ladder scrubbing like a maniac and sweating like a pig. It's only the middle of June, but it's so hot that the other housekeepers are wearing tiny shorts and have rolled up the sleeves of their staff shirts. I'm standing on a rickety ladder and can't swat at the bugs that'll inevitably come after my tender city flesh, so I've had to layer up: pants tucked into thick socks, heavy lace-up boots, long-sleeve shirt tucked into black gloves, a bulky bug-net hat pulled tight around my face. I'm focused on my task, which is to make sure my windows are streak-free—because if they aren't, Henry's going to make me redo them—and half-wondering if I can cool my body temperature using only my mind. This is one of those jobs that make me question everything about my summer so far. It doesn't seem safe. I don't have a spotter, there's no one holding the ladder or passing the bucket up to me, and it's entirely possible it could get so hot that I faint, fall backward, and hit my head, or fall forward and through one of the panes of glass. This is where Henry is so intent on making the lodge look perfect—which is a Sisyphean task, truly, a losing battle—that he tends to ignore what is best for his staff. Still, I don't want to be the girl who says no; I don't want to be the paranoid one.

I don't hear Jack's approach; I jump and wobble, swearing richly in shock. When I look down, he's standing on the ground behind my ladder.

"The highest . . . *what*?"

He scrutinizes my outfit. "Jesus Christ, Big Rig. Not a good look, eh?"

I imagine dumping the bucket of hot water on his face. I'm too grumpy for this: I'm so goddamned damp from the heat, every piece of clothing sticking to me, creating a terrible cocoon. I slither gracelessly down the ladder, clutching at the metal behind me, my heavy boots catching on every step. With inept, gloved hands, I rip the bug hat up so it gathers on the top of my head, black bridal veil revealing my irritated frown, so I can glare at him properly.

It's not my fault I look so awful; I'm trying to protect myself from the terrifyingly big horseflies, which I thought were wasps for the first few days because they're just as large and have similar striped bodies. Horseflies, from what I've heard, yank chunks out of you. They take their time to land and bite, and those bites throb like hives. I've never heard so many screamed expletives as I have when the housekeepers dart away from the horseflies when doing chores that force them to use their arms and hands for any extended period of time, like pinning up laundry or carrying wood from one lot to another.

Jack clicks his spit. "Look, here's a little tip: just put your hand on the top of your head and keep your palm open, and catch them before they sting you." He grins, his canines flashing in the glare of the sun, and he strides away before I can ask him if this piece of northern wisdom is more horseshit than not. Instead, I picture throwing the bucket at him and watching it bounce off his head. All I can do is dip my rag in the water again, turn back around, and climb up the ladder to resume my awful, relentless task. When I'm absolutely sure he's gone, I try, for one moment, to rest my hand, palm up, on the top of my head, but my gloves are too heavy: if something alights, I can't feel it at all.

I'm in that position a few seconds later when Henry comes into view. He stops to stare at me. Wasn't he just talking to Pea in his office? I'm always amazed at how quickly he can move around camp, all-seeing and all-hearing, always on high alert and light on his feet. Henry looks up at me with the expression of a disappointed parent, and I drop my hand to my side guiltily.

"I'm going to go inside and check your windows from there," he says. "Hopefully there aren't any streaks." *Or you'll be redoing everything* is the unspoken sentiment hanging on the heated air. I nod, glad he can't see my mutinous expression under the dark netting. I can feel the horseflies bouncing off of my body; they're as frustrated as I am. When he leaves, I curse Jack under my breath as loudly as I dare, and swat at the insects in the stupidest action of futility.

This place is rife with bugs. We're under attack from enemies we can barely see, let alone battle. Aside from horseflies, this is the first time I've experienced real blackflies, and I can't help but remember that Wade Hemsworth song: "*The black-flies, the little blackflies / always the blackfly no matter where you go / I'll die with the blackfly a-pickin' my bones / In North Ontar-I-o-I-o, In North Ontar-i-o.*" As a kid, I watched that National Film Board short by Christopher Hinton and rolled my eyes at the image of the hapless narrator crawling through the forest, trying to escape the bugs. Now I'm that hapless narrator. I'm the one running to submerge myself in the lake up to my neck to avoid these awful, relentless, multitudinous fuckers. I scratch— or pat frantically, when trying specifically *not* to scratch—along to the frenzied, jigging tune that's always playing in my head. Here's why these bugs are so insidious: when blackflies bite, you don't necessarily feel it, but you start bleeding, because they slash at the skin of their targets with saw-edged mouthparts rather than just piercing the skin. Blackflies actually take a piece of your meat. Many times I reach up to my ear to scratch or to brush my hair away from the nape of my neck and my hand comes away with red, wet fingertips. "Your face is bleeding" becomes a camp refrain. Still, the blood-dotted trail of the black-flies isn't as annoying to me as the needy whine of mosquitoes, their greedy bodies clustered on the bug nets around our bunks. Between one and the other, I'm constantly scratching at my skin, nails digging into lumps and bumps that turn raw and red with my ministrations.

And if the real, tangible insects aren't bad enough, Syd claims she sees "a demon bug" on our cabin wall one morning.

"Well, what did it look like?" We're curious, scared.

"Like a . . . bug! A beetle! With red eyes."

"Glowing red eyes?" I laugh.

"Shut up, man. It scared the shit out of me."

As we giggle, I can't help but look around at Emma and Robin and Syd. On our breaks, the sun, which turns fat and perfectly ripe only for a few perfect afternoon hours, spreads its fingers even all the way through the dark woods, and miraculously reaches the one dirty window of the back girls cabin. The heat warms up all of the conifers, and that perfect, raw, sugary smell rises and curls around our window screen. We're all smiling, relaxed, at home, and the soft edges of their three faces reflect the amber light. I can smell the good smells: pine needles; unwashed female bodies; fish-scale musk from inside and outside the boundaries of skin. I can hear the good sounds: our laughs, which have a sweet, dark edge that didn't exist before we got here; the creak of the bench as we rock back and forth and joke at Syd's expense; the whisper of the trees and also the silence of the woods behind us. We reach out and touch one another with pheromones; we roll our shoulders at the same time; we're becoming a cabal.

* * *

Even coming up on the halfway point of the summer, it's still sometimes easy to think that we're the only ones on this land. It's typical human egoism to believe that the world revolves around us weak, noisy humans, and that we're the top of the food chain. And while species diversity drops off the farther north you travel—a large portion of the Canadian taiga supports only 45 mammalian species; in comparison, Mexico supports 150, Costa Rica 163—up here, we're definitely not alone, nor are we the masters of our domain. Aside from the insects, we also live alongside beavers, muskrats, coyotes, wolves, deer mice, martens, foxes, little brown bats, black bears, moose, hares, caribou, chipmunks; we're thankfully a tiny bit too north for cougars and raccoons, and a little bit too south for polar bears. We have our regulars. There's a huge garter snake that lives under the concrete walkway to the lodge from the motel and suns itself on the path, scaring Alex every time she sees it; the angry red squirrels that eat mushrooms that grow in the forest and get stoned, screaming at us from the trees; and a groundhog we've named Chunk who hangs around the back door of the kitchen.

And then there's us. The filthiest, cruellest animals of all, bare-skinned weaklings who spend more time yelling at one another than is wise, who waste energy on stupid things like pleasure or reading or hanging out. We're a strange bunch, trying to eke out a summer together. But we're getting better at being with one another, and everyone is starting to go a little wild, deliciously, crazily so.

The mania spreads slowly, leaking out from my cabin and into the hands and veins and eyes of everyone else. Or maybe every cabin has its own core of frenzy, bred hot and compact, that grows with every wild laugh, every wild chore. Our group reversion starts at the breakfast table one morning, when Jack leans over to grab some more oatmeal and lets a fart rip. Not one of us blinks; a few of us even nod appreciatively. We slap at one another's asses and bellies, pass the bacon without lowering our cups of coffee from our mouths. "You still have crusty shit around your eyes," Robin howls. "I didn't sleep a good goddamn," Pete says. "Gee fucking whiz—ever loud thunder last night," Gus gripes. "Right over my head." We talk loose and easy: free, truly free, the small talk melted completely away as if it had been a piece of hard candy we'd been carrying around in the pouches of our cheeks. Now that the sugar is gone, the real taste comes through. And it's good. We're good without the saccharine niceties. We're better.

Our talk gets looser. We swear with more confidence and alacrity. We swear more creatively than we ever thought possible. The insults get meaner. The jokes get meaner. The jokes get dirtier. *I'll tell you how to have sex with a fat broad*, Gus says to us one night at dinner. *Roll her in flour and look for the wet spot.* And we all giggle, because we need to laugh to fuel our days, and so we do. It's times like these, when we're a pack around the staff table, relishing in something so incredibly politically incorrect that it wouldn't even make me smile back home, when I'm stunned at how lucky I am that I decided to apply for this job, and that I was hired.

There are many different reasons for a twentysomething to leave her life behind and come up north for a job like this one. For the dockhands and guides, this is often a career step to running their own outfit or going into competitive fishing. For the housekeepers, it seems to be something else altogether.

"I wanted to go on an adventure," Syd tells me. "Is that weird? That's my honest answer."

"Not weird," I say.

"I just thought it sounded wild, and I wanted to take off for the summer and be free. Adventure sounds cheesy, I know. But my older brother always went off on adventures in the summer and I wanted the same thing."

Robin uses strikingly similar language. "I thought it would be a good opportunity for some sort of summer adventure. Something new and completely out of my realm," she says. "I figured what the hell, why not? I didn't have anything at that point."

Still, this adventure can get overwhelming. Sometimes it's so much, all of this animal magnetism held captive in our small bodies and our small rooms. That's when some of us disappear. The veterans know the nooks and crannies; the rest of us have had to figure it out. The brave ones go to the dump to be alone. The canny ones manage to finagle chores—rock haul, buoy dropping—that require them to jet off in a boat for an entire afternoon. The taciturn ones stay in bed and zip their sleeping bags over their heads and yank down their bug nets. The green ones, like me, know nowhere else to go except the staff beach, and so that's where I head.

Standing on the shore, I close my eyes and breathe in and out. I'm not entirely alone: I can hear the on-shore guides yelling about firewood and tackle and chores and boats and motors. Their voices curve around the point that separates the staff beach from the guests' shoreline, and it's almost like they're right next to me, leering, laughing like they always do.

I peel off my uniform and hold it to my face for a moment; it smells like oily hair and greasy skin, the result of only being able to wash my clothes once a week. We live in our own filth—the wax that skin creates from friction and sweat; the crotches of pants that haven't been laundered in weeks—and therefore to smell our bodies clean is sometimes alien. Before coming up here, I might have found the scent of dirty human distressing, but now it's oddly comforting.

I walk into the shallows, leaving ripples of oil behind me, the remnants of bug spray and lotion and cooking grease that have accumulated on my skin throughout the week. As I slide my feet along the pebbly bottom, I keep my eyes down, looking for movement. Being in water makes me nervous; I'm out of my element, vulnerable. If I close my eyes, I can picture the lake full of fish, all of them staring at my pale legs. I wonder, irrationally, if pike would slide around my ankles like a cat might. Marking me with mucus. Marking me as their own. I walk farther, the water ringing my torso, lapping at the bottoms of my breasts, stealing the breath from my lungs. I lean my head back and feel the tips of my hair get heavy with water; I ease my body into the lake, part by part, until the water curls at my collarbone and I can slip under, running my fingertips across my scalp and across my eyebrows as I stretch under the surface.

It's times like these when I feel as though I could bring magic to my body. Being alone here stokes different emotions: either I feel panicky, uncomfortable without someone near me cracking jokes and touching me and being in complete close contact, or I feel powerful. Today, as exposed as I am, I feel like I could raise my hands and take the energy from this land, this mean, fierce land, and lace it throughout my body. I want to take this place with me and keep it forever, put it into the bones of my pelvis and the skin on the soles of my feet. I'm on the cusp of some new form, a raw core of sexuality and power that exists in the stripped-down, scrubbed-off version of myself that is emerging day by day.

Caught in my own thoughts, idly touching my hip bones and waist, the water rocking against my knees and the pale insides

of my thighs, I remember something Jack told the girls on our
first day.

"For chrissake," he said. "Your painted toenails probably
look just like fishing lures."

I think I feel something slide up against my ankle. Fierceness
is momentarily forgotten as I kick up my heels and run back
to the beach, water slicing around me as I lurch, laughing and
laughing and laughing.

●　●　●

One afternoon, I'm pulled out of a face-down nap by a dull
buzzing. I come slowly out of sleep, confused and drooling a
little. As I raise my head, I try to assess the sound. It could be
anything—a Whippersnipper, a boat motor, a faraway chainsaw. But as I shift from asleep to nearly awake, I feel a vibration,
something that pushes up against my white bug net. I squint.
Three fat bumblebees float thickly on the air, circling.

I rip my net back and dart from my bed, ducking through
their invisible sign of infinity. I pull on a pair of shorts and a thin
tank top, for a little decency, and open the cabin door, stumbling
out into the forest and right into Jack's path.

"Help me," I sputter, bare-legged and dumb-mouthed. My
tongue feels swollen with sleep, my eyes sandy. It's so goddamned quiet. The generator seems to be off, probably for
refuelling, and I can't hear anybody else. Where is everyone?
Where are the girls in my cabin? If I had to guess, I'd say the
others are out having a lake shower, or sitting on the shoreline
writing letters, or maybe watching old movies on VHS in the

main building, but it feels wrong to be alone, like everyone flew back home and somehow Jack and I are the only ones left. Maybe I'm half-asleep; my brain feels cloudy and strange. I'm hot and also clammy, and I rub my upper arms with my hands to create some friction and also to try to cover my chest in the bright beam of the afternoon light.

Despite my vague two-word bleat, Jack doesn't hesitate—he slips inside our cabin, dark hands in front of him and at the ready. I wonder if he's curious about what he's walking into. It could be anything: a bear at the window, a snake in the bed, a leak in the roof. My bees will seem stupid in comparison to any of these, but I can't bring myself to smack them down. It's so much easier to get help, to be a little bit weak in this moment. As I follow him, I'm immediately conscious of the way our living space smells so very female, like salt and dirt and that odd, deep smell that women get when they don't wash their hair every day. It smells like our sleep, our bodies, our beings, maybe even our dreams, and I turn pink.

Jack looks around perfunctorily, noticing the pictures of shirtless men we have taped up on our wall. Of course he hasn't been in here this year—the back girls cabin of this cohort was probably a bit of a mystery to him.

"Nice art, eh," he murmurs.

"Shut up," I whisper.

The bumblebees hum in the air around us.

"This what you need help with, Big Rig?" He jerks his thumb at the bugs. "Why don't you just roll up one of those dumb magazines and kill them?" He gestures to the *Cosmopolitans* on the table.

"I don't want to kill them. I just want them out of the cabin."
He gives me an odd look. "All right."

I spend the next few minutes watching Jack cup his hands
around the bees, crooning at them in a low and patient voice.
Come on, big girl, come on, pretty, he says, jerking his head at
me when he wants me to open the door and when he wants me
to keep it closed. *Shush, shush*, he says, ushering the bugs out of
the cabin one by one, and then he leaves. I don't say thank you
and he doesn't expect it.

● ● ●

Throughout the summer, guides are flown in for stints of various lengths. During the busier times, Henry tries to have as
many men on hand as possible to take guests out on the lake.
Later this summer, we'll meet Cedric, a pewter artisan who
runs his own fishing outfit most of the year. And Murphy, the
gruff, bearded guide who looks like Hemingway and is nick-
named Chief Stormcloud by the dockhands because he calls all
the young men "peckerheads" and goes to bed at 9 p.m., getting
grumpy if anyone in camp dares to be audibly rowdy after his
bedtime. And Max, well into his eighties and still going strong.
I fished with Max last summer. He's my father's favourite guide
because of his gentle nature, his patience, and his sneaky sense
of humour. Max can get a line into the water faster than anybody I've ever seen; he can tie knots one-handed and still drive
a boat with the other hand.

Sometimes, guides come in for most of the summer, unable
to swing the whole nine weeks because of other commitments

but not willing to say no to time up north; this is the case with Wade, a quiet hunk of a man from Lion's Head who flew into Kesagami a couple of weeks after we arrived. When he landed, the girls were lined up on the dock waiting for the groceries to be unloaded, so we didn't notice the tall figure unfolding himself from the front seat. Then one of the housekeepers elbowed another, hard bone wedged into soft breasts and tight ribs, and jabs and nudges and hissed words travelled down the line, our eyes widening and our postures improving as he made his way up the dock to the shore.

Wade is a catalyst. He turns the housekeepers into some rom-com version of themselves: whenever he enters a room, the female staff members sigh like some corny chorus; whenever he smiles, with that kind of male half-smirk that makes women fan themselves and rub their thighs together, the girls bite their lips and have to look away for fear of being teased by the other boys. Robin, who up until now hasn't shown any interest in hanging around the male staff cabins, seems to be spending more time in that quadrant of camp. Quiet Emma ends up persuading Wade to give her a ride on his shoulders back to her cabin one night; I watch as she furrows her fingers into his blond hair and shrieks as he sprints along the back path.

Wade's easy to get along with, rolls with the punches, and he's also somehow kind. He never bullies the girls, doesn't prod at us until we cry, stays quiet when the other guys are causing a ruckus. This could be because he didn't join the pack at the very beginning. Maybe he hasn't had enough time to learn how to get under our skin, or feels that he doesn't have the right. Maybe, because he's twenty-nine, older than the rest of us, he feels above it. Conversely, we won't have a chance to get to know his character flaws, or really get to know him as well as we know each other, because he'll be flown out of camp a couple of weeks before the rest of us.

Wade's presence amps everything up: a new man is a new choice in our games of Fuck, Marry, Kill that we play on our afternoons off. We figure out that it's better to embrace the animal than to fight it. We start ranking one another in terms of attractiveness. We discuss our bathroom habits more often than is necessary, often over lunch. We want meat. We want alcohol. We want to masturbate—preferably in private, but we'll do it among our sleeping roommates if need be. These are topics and urges and conversations that have little to no place in the real world. But here, the rudeness I repress in my normal life pours out of me. It pours out of all of us. This is no-man's land. No-woman's land, too.

And at the end of our day, we slink through the door of the guideshack in shifts. We flop onto the bench by the fire, or burrow into one of the guides' beds if it's been a particularly bad night shift. There's also bootleg alcohol in the guideshack: half-bottles of rye gifted to us by understanding guests, leftover cans of Molson snatched by housekeepers from empty cabins. Sometimes, we pool our money and ask obliging guests to buy a case of beer for us—but not too often, because two-fours of beer cost seventy-five dollars up here. We scrounge and save, and on some nights we have wild, short-shift parties before stumbling off to bed. Gus keeps a mini-fridge in his bunk, and on the good nights, the Coors Light and the Canadian cans roll out fresh and frosty, and we share them back and forth. This is how so many of us end up hungover on some mornings. It's also how so many of us get sick in waves of group phlegm and sticky shared fever. But those repercussions don't matter when we're piled in, five to a bunk, listening to bad, loud dance music and swigging shit beer. This is the way we slough off the stresses of the day.

During one of these get-togethers, my camera goes missing and I'm frothy with panic. I have so many pictures and videos on there, artifacts I'm not ready to lose. Tiff steps up, walking me along the paths between cabins and up and down the staff beach, where we scour the ground, our eyes straining in the wavering dusk light. When we return to the guideshack, me close to tears of frustration, Gus comes out of his bunk with my camera.

"Where did you get that?" I'm not even accusatory, just so relieved to see it. I feel like I could cry, but I don't want the dockhands and guides to see me lose it over something as small as this.

"I found it wedged between my mattress and the wall. It must have fallen out of your pocket when you were in my bunk or something," he says, handing it back to me. The story checks out: Gus is the keeper of the beer and we spend a lot of time in his room.

I lurch at him, wrap my arms around his body, and hug him as tightly as I can, mumbling *thank you thank you thank you* under my breath.

A day later, I flip the camera on. Alex has been looking over my shoulder, and her scream can be heard from the shoreline all the way to Cabin 6.

The photos are crude boy photos—bums and hairy chests, a couple of testicles from where a few of the dockhands leaned over too far when posing with their asses out. There's even a picture of one of them basically pulling his asshole open. I smack a hand over my eyes, groaning, peeking through my fingers. As I flick through the pictures, I realize that I never lost the camera; somehow, the guys grabbed it when I wasn't looking, whether it was slipped out of my pocket or swiped from a bench, and booby-trapped it with half-naked snapshots. And then Gus lied so smoothly and convincingly that I fell for it, hook, line, and sinker. I'm partly angry, partly amazed at what a team of sneaks they are, that none of the girls noticed. I wince at a picture of three of them all bent over with their ass cheeks out.

And then I get to the last photo.

"What is this?" My voice has reached a melodramatic shriek-pitch, but I can't help it. Alex is in shock beside me. She's shaking her head. "*Who is this?*"

Whoever the boy is has pulled his penis back between his legs and pushed his thighs together, so his crotch looks vaguely like a woman's. There aren't any distinguishing characteristics. I try not to look too hard. All I can see is that the pubic hair is dark.

Tiff scuttles over, peering at the screen. Her voice changes as soon as she sees the picture. I can hear the hardness in her throat—it comes up to her eyes when she turns to look at me.

"Those are Jack's boxers." Each word is clipped.

"They stole the camera," I say, immediately, defensively.

Tiff's lips tighten.

"Fucking animals."

•   •   •

The next time I go for a swim, I walk out as quickly as I can and drop to my knees. I put my head underwater and feel this odd fever ebb for a moment, and then I scream, mouth full of water, as loud as I can, as long as I can, until I have no more breath.

NAIADS

On nights when the weather is good and the bugs aren't too bad, when we finish dinner service before the sun goes down, and we're not too stressed from serving the guests, we spend part of the evening on the staff beach, watching the dark slide in across the water. We can't be out for too long, since sound travels and the fishermen in the cabins nearby are bedding down, but we cobble together a small fire, warm our hands and the soles of our feet as the night deepens around our bodies, and watch the sky go from powder periwinkle to a deep and dusty blue, rich and dark and foreboding.

Tonight, I'm wading in the shallows, just far enough that the water comes to the knobby bones of my ankles. The lake exhales around me, slowly calming from its day. The stars are starting to poke out, and the treetops stroke the sky as though feeling for the residual warmth from the melting sundown. For a moment, I feel like the conductor of an orchestra, as if I could lift my hands and everything in front of me might respond to my ticking fingers. I put my hand in front of my face and my fingers disappear into the background of the black lake in just a few blinks of my eyes, until it's suddenly so dark I'm sure I'm just a murky silhouette against the horizon.

Behind me, the girls are roasting marshmallows, painting their toenails, hissing at one another, ripping into care packages sent from home. I turn my head and watch them, witnessing what the guests have seen this summer. We have become one great machine: we move—pass, smile, insult—as a group, our motions a guileless choreography of comfort.

Sometimes, something about the nuances of woman-to-woman interaction is lost on me; I don't understand the bowing and bobbing of heads, the hierarchy, the need to compliment and not accept compliments in return. So the fact that I have seven new girlfriends—bred from nothing but sweat, proximity, and the ability to humble ourselves—is stunning. As I look at them, I feel gratitude so intense it wraps its hands around my guts and squeezes, and my eyes well up and the fire blurs. I'm so glad it's dark and no one can see me tearing up on the shoreline, watching these nymphs weave arms around one another and laugh with the clear, cutting trill of water between fingers and stars in the sky.

They are a frieze, perfection—Robin and Syd and Emma searching for good sticks, Aubrey and Alex and Alisa whittling, Tiff craning her neck to see if her marshmallow is golden or on the edge of burnt. The men are on the fringes, partly in the dark, and it's the women who shine. I gaze at each of them and their faces are lit up with the warm amber glow.

ALISA

Alisa and I lie in Kevin's bed. Pea is sitting across from us, on an unused lower bunk. He's taking pictures as we paw through Kev's clothing, fishing out lush woollen sweaters and neon-coloured long johns. Alisa giggles as we pull on his shirts and roll around in his flannel sheets. Head by head, our blonde and red mixes in eddies, and he'll be finding long hairs on his pillow for days to come.

Jack appears at the doorway and Alisa looks up. "What do you want?"

Wordlessly, he sticks his ass into the room and farts, and then uses a Rubbermaid bin lid he had hidden by the wall to fan it at us aggressively.

Alisa and I scream, laughing, and it's at that moment that Pea takes another photo and we are memorialized—arms around each other, mid-shriek, eyes half-closed and angled to Jack, who is standing out of the frame, to the side.

ROBIN

Robin is quieter than the rest of the girls, and that's why I like her so much. She's broad-shouldered and strong, and because of this Henry "volunteers" her for some of the tougher jobs, all of which she does without complaint. It's not surprising to see her mowing the lawn, or using a Whippersnipper to trim the edging along the path—jobs that no other housekeeper dares to take on. She also has a funny habit of breaking everything she touches: toilets, sinks, wheelbarrows. It's not that she's clumsy, just that the pieces seem to fall apart in her hands. We joke that she has bad luck, and she jokes along with us, too, but I think it takes a toll on her.

I think Robin feels as if she's on the periphery, that she doesn't quite fit in with the rest of the girls and that maybe she should. I like the things that set her apart: her willingness to work hard, the fact that she doesn't run her mouth or talk about inane things. When something goes wrong, she doesn't offer up stupid advice for the sake of talking. Instead, she sits and listens.

So I'm glad it's her who I find when I burst into the lodge, hot-faced and manic, holding two pillowcases in my hands.

"I need help," I say.

I can't remember how to fold the linens the way we've been taught. Normally, I love laundry days: the laundry room is so isolated from the rest of the camp that to work in it all day is to isolate oneself, too. The dull thrum of the washing machines can be soothing, and the room is warm and low-ceilinged, always damp because it's located partly underground beneath the motel. There are bottles of cleaning products on the dusty wooden shelves, and, in the very back, there's a storage room that hasn't been excavated in years. When some of the housekeepers peek back there, we find a child's fishing rod from the 1990s, and a mesh baseball cap with a lodge logo from long before that.

Today I'm panicky. This is not how I expected my breakdown to happen. Each of us is due for an emotional routing, and sometimes the smallest things are the triggers. So far I've seen Kevin lose it over good-natured ribbing by the girls, Emma crumple into tears over an unwashed plate waiting for her in the dishpit, Sydney lose her cool over the stressful nature of steak night. Running on so little sleep, completely emotionally peeled as we are, some days are generally weepy. I didn't expect that laundry was going to be my thing.

Robin walks me back to the laundry room, grabbing my damp hand as soon as we're out of sight of the lodge. It seems like such a small kindness, but it's so large in that moment. I lose my words, and press the clean sheets to my face. I cry into the linens, my shoulders hunched, vibrating with the frustrations of shitty sleeps and sexual tension and feeling geographically helpless. Robin doesn't say anything silly. All she does is put a hand between my shoulder blades. Standing beside me, leaning against the chest freezer, so close our bodies touch, she guides me through the different ways to fold the linens. When I've calmed, she crushes my shoulders in a reassuring sidelong squeeze, and leaves to continue watching her movie.

AUBREY

Aubrey sits beside me at the staff dinner table; we're chewing miniature pizzas as fast as we can, taking huge bites and trying to scarf down as much food as possible before it's time to go back to work. She's wearing a lodge jacket from the 1980s to keep pizza sauce from getting all over her serving whites. I grin at her, tomato sauce caught between my teeth.

"Little Henrys," she says with a moan through a full mouth. That's what these pizzas are called, disturbingly—Little Henrys, like our boss. They're about a billion calories apiece, but they're so good we beg Sam to make them at least twice a week. Tonight, he's acquiesced, and Aubrey and I are making the most of it by shoving them into our mouths before the real Henry slides back in and extricates us.

Aubrey's mostly quiet and judicious in a way that makes her seem stilted at first, so it took me longer to get to know her. She speaks slowly to get her point across; she makes important observations. On her afternoons off, she'd rather take a canoe out with Wade or Pea—and not just for a half-assed ride along the shore. They go on adventures, genuine paddles, because that's where Aubrey releases her stress, in nature, away from camp and away from the shenanigans.

Still, there are times when she'll say something so funny, so out of the blue and spot on, and those are the moments I feel closest to her, when she lets loose her unexpected, rich blare of a laugh.

Pea walks in and tosses Aubrey a potato. "From the dockhands," he says.

The potato is heart-shaped, and carved into it is "WE LOVE U GUYS." She starts laughing, and I can't help but join in.

ALEX

Alex walks into the staff dining room as I'm sitting, reading and eating a piece of buttered bread.

"What are you doing?"

"Nothing really," I say.

Something about her movement distracts me from my book, and so I take a better look at her. She's unfocused, her lanky body unusually heavy. Her movements are manifested in subtle but distressed tics.

"What's wrong?"

She's still for a moment. The two of us are suspended in a tableau of in-between before she finally speaks. "My sister phoned and told me to phone her back right away. And now I can't get in touch with her." I realize, suddenly, that Alex is beyond panic, and that's why I didn't immediately identify her upset: she's in that deep stage of terror. "It's my family. I know it is. I think—" She stops. I stare, not wanting to move for fear of scaring her off. "Maybe one of my parents died."

It seems like a dramatic jump, but it's not. Because we're so isolated, it takes time for news of home to reach us, and so it's easy to think the worst. My body tenses. There's nothing I can say, no platitudes that will ease her anxiety. The only thing to do is to wait for the satellites to shift back into alignment and to stay with her while she phones home—if that's what she wants.

Later, when Alex sits at the phone and learns that it's her grandfather who passed away, she sobs so hard that her body shakes, the kind of weeping where sound doesn't even come out, not even tears, just harsh, jolting movements. I try to wrap myself around her. It's not a gesture that takes any thought, just a warm animal instinct of trying to protect one of my own.

"Yes," Alex says to her sister. "No. I'm not alone."

SYDNEY

"Look!"

Syd has her camera in her hand, and she's waving it back and forth, ambling toward me down the motel hallway. She's in charge of cleaning the bathrooms today, and I'm on my way to bring some towels to room number eight.

"Oh no."

"You wanna know what I've been doing today?" Her eyes glitter in the dim motel light.

"Did you . . . bring your camera to clean rooms?"

"*Do you wanna know what I've been doing today?*"

I already have a pretty good idea of what she's been doing today, because I also do it every week, but I start giggling immediately. "What have you been doing today?"

"Cleaning up *shit*." She emphasizes the last word so heavily it sounds like *shet*. "Pubic . . . scrubbed . . . like, the *shit* out of everything." Pubic scrub is not a technical term in the housekeeping lexicon, but I know exactly what she means. Sometimes the toilets and the showers get to such a state that we're not sure if the men are shedding or just pulling their own hair out and spattering it on the ceramic.

"Look," she says, switching on the camera and flipping through a few photos. I'm doing that kind of laughing where I'm keeping my mouth closed to try to stave it off, but it's escaping anyway, in high-pitched nasal squeaks.

"Why do you have your camera?"

"Every time I find a bad shit stain on one of the toilets, I take a photo of it."

"Wh—"

"Because I want to remember the fucking work I'm doing here! Because no one will *believe* me when I tell them!" With that, she turns the camera around and shows me what's on her screen. My mouth falls open. "How do you even *do* that?"

I can't help it. I start laughing so hard that I have to bend over to try to keep it from tearing me open with its strength.

She's still attempting to keep the camera in my sightline, and I'm trying to wave it away.

"*How?*"

I grab at her body from where I'm doubled over. I paw at her thighs and her stomach and her waist, trying to anchor myself. But it's no use; she's taken my legs out from under me, with just one interaction, one picture, and I'm floating away, carried on a ream of lawless, lusty laughter that can only come from being completely comfortable with another person. She can't help it: she starts, too, her indignation melting a little bit.

"*How?!*"

EMMA

Emma and I sleep close together in the top bunks, and because of this, we share a strange bond, a connection forged in the intimate, fuzzy moments as we nod off and right after waking up. She is so different from me—younger, fair, petite, immature in a way that I know will even out once she figures out who she is and what she wants. We are close to being complete opposites, save for our fierce senses of humour.

One night, I bundle myself into my sleeping bag and say my goodnights to her through the double mesh of our bug nets.

"Blue jean baby," she murmurs back.

"What?" I roll over to face her, frowning. "Oh no."

Sydney joins in the song from the bunk below me and I groan, my visions of an early bedtime evaporating. She sings the next line with such a warble that I'm sure Robin is now awake, if she wasn't before. "Shut up," I say, somewhere between good-natured and exhaustedly fed up.

"Ballerina—" This is belted out from Robin's bunk, and I know she's been awake this whole time. Their three voices are so very different, but together they are a beautiful chorus, even bone-dead tired and lying in their dirty sleeping bags, their voices filtered through netting. My irritation is gone because how can it not be? I'm caught in the web of their song, and I'm smiling.

"Here it comes," Emma hollers, suddenly sitting up in bed, and I start to laugh outright in anticipation until the chorus of "Tiny Dancer" finally rolls around and I join in, my mouth half-hidden in my pillow, my voice not as strong as their voices—but the four of us sound better than any concert, and I wonder if the bears, the wolves, the sleeping crows can hear us from wherever they are.

"You had a busy day today."

TIFF

Tiff cradles a mickey of rum in her arms as the housekeepers stand on the beach, our heads craned as far back as we can manage.

"Show us the North Star!"

"Show us the planets!"

She motions with one arm, and, to me, she could be pointing at anything. The sky is filled with stars, a depthless well of wishes that probably never came to fruition but still glow with conviction anyway. Away from the light and the pollution of cities, the constellations shiver and stretch, taking up more of the sky than their boundaries should allow. We follow the arc of Tiff's finger, looking from one pearled point to another, our necks burning, our arms looped around each other's waists and shoulders.

"That's the Big Dipper," she says in that placid, beautiful voice, the voice that calms the most truculent personalities in camp, that guides us through the stressful prime rib dinner service, that coaches us in our hospital corners and pillow plumping.

"We know that!"

"We're not stupid!"

Actually, we might be a bit stupid, especially when it comes to the stars, but Tiff only smiles kindly and continues pointing.

"The Little Dipper," she says, tracing the shape with her finger.

"Okay, okay!"

She continues, naming constellations like she's reciting some sort of heavenly spell, words like *Lyra, Hercules, Draco, Aquila*. She's never impatient, making sure our heads follow wherever she's gesturing to, our eyes wide and our mouths wider.

I know absolutely nothing about what I'm looking at. But we're together, filling the quiet with our sounds, and even though there's no fire to keep the bugs away, even though we're supposed to be in bed and we're going to be exhausted come morning, we don't want to leave the beach for bunks. I could stay out here all night.

We stand up from the cold sand and jig to keep warm. We take on the greens and blacks of the night glow, the skin of our faces and the backs of our hands alive with the light of the stars and the yawn of the moon. We spin. We spin and spin until we can't tell the difference between the two sides of the horizon, until we drop. Until the biggest adventure we can manage is trying to find each other's bodies in the dark and hold on tight until we can't laugh anymore.

*   *   *

The girls decide to go swimming one evening. The boys are still pulling boats, and we don't have the patience to wait for them. The sun is setting, and the lake is so still that it looks like a golden scrying pool. By some lovely fluke, it's a beautiful almost-dusk: the perfect temperature, and the sky, clear and orange and red, is a bowl without boundary.

We drag a canoe onto the water. Some of us perch in the boat, and some of us swim alongside to pull it. We wait for the boys to realize that we're missing; I know that once they've done the pull, they'll come and find us. They'll grab our clothes from the shoreline and roar at us to emerge from the water so they can ogle. We'll ignore them, flicking our hair and turning our backs.

I plant my feet on the sandy bottom and look into the dipping sun. I'm so lucky to be here. The feeling strikes me like a bolt that goes all the way to my core and settles there. The thankfulness is so acute it hurts. Somehow, we've forged a family. We've cleverly forgotten about differences that would be glaring back in the default world. Being away from the things that we thought defined us, working hard and showering less, doesn't make us less human. Somehow, it makes us even more human.

Beside me, there's an unsteady shriek in the canoe. I look over and watch as the boat totters back and forth, on the edge of capsizing. Emma falls out, her pale, slim legs flying up into the air as she plunges under. Alisa, who is sitting on the gunwale, leans her head back and guffaws like a cartoon character, but doesn't realize that this changes the weight of the canoe, and then she is falling backward, too, still giggling as her blonde head goes under. The girls who threw their towels in the canoe cluck, but the scene is too funny not to smile. The overturned boat sits like a giant fish beside us, hull glowing and exhaling and inhaling with the gentle movement of the water.

I tilt my face to the sun and realize that this is the most beautiful thing I've ever seen. Setting on the straight, bright edge of the horizon, the sun looks like a seed ready to explode. We're in the water at the exact right time. In only a few minutes, the lake will become fire, and when we slide into a breaststroke and dip our heads under the water, we will be diving into sheer orange and red and gold gloss, frothing the glass surface of the water up into a spray of opaline glow. We will be alight.

I take my bathing suit off, feeling the water rush over my stomach and my shoulders and the curve of my hips. The other girls whoop and whistle, and some take their suits off too. We hear the boys crashing through the camp toward us. And then we all cock our heads to the side, uncanny and ready and smiling. Slip under the water at the same time, sleek naiads in the glow.

SAM

The lodge kitchen is an intimate space, so crowded that girls often have to sidle past each other, feeling the press of pelvises and breasts to backs, murmuring softly when the heat of bodies connects. This room is the true heart of the lodge. It's the place where the girls come together every morning and night, where we sweat and swear in our efforts to get the guests fed and watered in time for a day out on the lake or in time for bed. The servers and Sam, the cook, pull off miracles every day, all in this tiny area.

The dishpit is where the kitchen's in-door is located. Servers burst in and dump guests' sticky, used plates and cutlery onto the housekeeper on dish duty, who's usually silently ruing her life choices while elbow deep in bleach water filled with scummy bowls and spoons and mugs. To hand off orders to Sam and pick up plates that are ready, servers have to move through the dishpit into the main kitchen, an area that's really not much bigger than the back girls cabin. There are two huge fridges against one wall, and the range against the other. To top it off, a sharp-cornered metal table occupies most of the middle of the room. Because the kitchen is so small, it's a stressful place full of complex timing and choreography. There are different cuts of meat that need to be cooked to different desires; different pans of eggs that need to be turned into scrambled, sunny side up, over medium; young women spinning around one another, their ponytails whipping behind them. But no matter what's going on, no matter how chaotic, everyone is aware that the entire kitchen is Sam's domain, from one end to the other, up and down, every shelf, pot, rack, spatula, and knife.

We were warned that Sam has a particular brand of emotional hazing that he inflicts on the housekeepers.

"Just show him your mettle," Jack said. "Tell him 'bring it on!' and he'll probably respect you. You'll have to do a lot of dishes, but he'll respect you. Probably."

"No," Tiff said. "You just want to avoid eye contact. Bring your headphones with you on dishpit days."

"It starts off fine," Alex said. "But then it's not."

"I like him," Kevin said. "He gives me brownies."

"This is my third year here," Alex continued with an eye roll, "and he still calls me *that girl*."

* * *

Each day is made up of a chain of tasks, and that's how time pulls us through even when our bodies are weary and we feel like we're about to break down. We survive by counting the minutes from one chore to the other, relishing the work we like and grumbling through the work we hate. We all have favourite duties. I still look forward to laundry days the most: it's a day to hide and read, sitting cross-legged on top of the dryer as I wait for my towels to be done. Other girls like bartending, because it's the only day we're able to sleep past 6 a.m., or they like serving, slinging salads and rolls and testing their memories by remembering guests' orders without a notepad. For all of our differences, though, there's one common denominator—nobody likes dishpit.

Even though the camp has a capacity for a maximum of sixty guests—and twenty staff members, give or take—we don't have an industrial dishwasher, so all the dishes are done by hand by one girl. Every pot, pan, plate, piece of cutlery is washed with soap first, then bleach water, and finally rinsed in hot water. Everything is hand-dried, put back on the shelves, and then used again within thirty minutes. Wash. Repeat. All day, every day, from breakfast service at 7 a.m. to the end of dinner service around 9 p.m.

"It's hard," I tell Pea. We're sitting beside each other on a hot afternoon, watching Jack as he sorts his tackle box. I know that Pea knows working with Sam is hard; he's been a dockhand for years, he's heard it all. But I can't help but unleash a little. "It's the hardest work I've ever done. And Sam is so . . . " I'm paranoid about saying anything too loudly, since sound carries and I never know anyone's whereabouts.

I press my hands to my eyes. I'm not crying, but I'm not okay, either. It seems like Sam is getting worse by the week, as if he plans how best to break down every girl's brave facade with every dishpit day. In the first weeks of the summer, he was giving us the normal things to wash, just pans and tongs and forks.

It was hard, but it was predictable. Then, he asked us to wash pieces of the range that we've never seen before, metal that was black and burnt from years of use. Then, he asked us to mop the kitchen three or four times a day, wanted us to beat the filthy mats over the clothesline in the glare of the midday sun. Then, he asked us to kneel in the corners of the kitchen, using our bleach-ragged nails to pry dirt out of the space where the floor meets the wall. Now it's an intense sense of dread every time I wake up on a Thursday morning and realize it's my day in the pit.

I only have about thirty minutes with the guys before I have to go back in. I'm worried and overtired, and I should be lying down and saving my strength for the impending dinner service. Normally I'd try to nap, but it's sweltering today; the heat is so unctuous and presses so hard on the napes of our necks that Pea and I loll our heads, trying to catch as much wind off the lake as possible. The heat seems to have slowed him down, a rare sight, and his taciturn nature has melted a bit.

"You're lucky this year," Pea says, his words slow like he's chewing.

"Why?"

Before Pea can answer, Jack bends over to pick up a lure he's dropped on the bottom of his boat, and his shirt rides up, exposing his ass crack.

"You need a new belt," I yell, but the air is so thick it feels like the words just hang there.

"Fuck you, Big Rig," he hollers back in a sing-song way. "Don't look at my ass."

"I've literally already seen it," I snap.

"Yeah? Did you see any willnots?"

Pea starts shaking with laughter beside me.

"What. The fuck. Is. A willnot?" I wish my words were harsher, but I'm too tired to give them the bite I want.

Jack straightens himself and grins. "A ball of shit, stuck in your ass hair, that willnot come out, no matter how much you wipe!" He looks like he expects a drum rimshot to accompany what he clearly thinks is a very funny joke.

I clap both hands to my eyes again, as if I'd be able to shield myself from that image by blocking out the visual of Jack laughing, his big teeth clicking and catching the sun. "No!"

"No what? No, you didn't see any? Bet you looked pretty hard, eh, Big Rig?"

Pea's full-out guffawing. I turn back to him, eager to change the subject. "Why am I lucky? When it comes to Sam?"

"In the past," he says, swallowing another laugh, "Sam's been so much worse. He hasn't made anyone cry this summer, has he?"

"Don't think so," I say. "At least not face to face."

"He used to be . . . bad. He used to be pretty bad."

"Oh, yeah," Jack pipes up, laying a few lures on his boat seats. I watch his long fingers as he sorts through the tackle. A bead of sweat starts from my hairline and rolls down my spine, getting absorbed in the waist of my shorts.

I should be happy that Jack is being fairly nice to me. Today is a good day. Some days, the way he talks to me is so jarring: "Heya, Big Rig! You fucking up your chores again or what?" "Jesus, Big Rig. We could use you as a dockhand instead of goddamned Aidan. Aidan, you big fucking idiot, look at how much weight Big Rig can move in her wheelbarrow!" "Big Rig sucks,

Big Rig sucks, fuck you, Big Rig!—" sung along aggressively to a strummed guitar in the guideshack.

Our interactions are mostly like brother and sister. We needle, him far more expertly than me, but there's an undercurrent of something else, something mean and proud, something that makes me uncomfortable in a sick, pleasurable way. I make no mistake about Jack: his curiosity about me, if it exists at all, is tainted with a deep dislike of my city life ("Fucking Toronto. Shit drivers, shit people"), of my arts degree ("Might as well be doing arts and crafts, Big Rig"), of my potential for brittleness ("I usually make at least one housekeeper cry by this point in the summer. Wonder when it's going to be your turn, huh?"), but most of all, I think, my refusal to bend to him. There's a rage we seem to bring out in each other, but it's balanced by the fact that no one on staff makes me laugh as hard as he does. His humour is brutal, clever, exquisite in a rapid-fire way; he makes jokes at everyone's expense, and all I can do is breathe deeply and let myself be carried by the waves of invective. If you're good to Jack, he will keep you grinning; if you're on the outs with Jack, he will punish you.

Pea looks at me, and I realize that I've been staring. I snap my attention back to him, his sweaty eyebrows, the sheen on his cheekbones and chin. It's so fucking hot. He puts his hand on my shoulder; I can feel his heat, and I close my eyes. Maybe I'm understanding him a little better; he's older than even me, has worked alongside years of idiots, I'm sure. Pea toils hard, quietly, usually without complaint, and he expects the rest of us to do the same. The housekeepers' mouthy languor—that delicious cruelty that most young women inherit from society, from fear, from pack mentality—is naturally annoying to him. I think he wonders why we all can't scrub, hammer, chop, rake, haul without whining, without unleashing. But Pea is the aberration; his stoicism makes him the reliable one, but it also sets him apart when we're running wild and giddy. He does unwind, though; he likes rum, likes a good dirty joke, delivers one-liners with a quiet confidence that keeps his audience silent and thinking for a moment before the joke truly lands and we catch up and gasp with laughter.

I make a sound with my throat, thankful for this moment of quiet. I want this lull to continue; it feels like we're stuck in a delicious bubble, our limbs weighed down with the curtain of heat. If I had my way, I'd spend all summer like this, propped up under a tree, exchanging gentle banter with men who know far more than me about this place and this history.

"You'll be okay," Pea says, and I nod with my eyes closed.

＊　＊　＊

Sam's face slants forward. His hair is silvering, his shoulders sloped. His arms and legs are skinny, but he's solid around the middle. His physicality doesn't add up. He moves in tics and bursts, energy propelling its way out of him through herky-jerky movements. Any time he's feeling awkward, he snaps his head back and laughs as loud and hard as he can to the ceiling while holding a soup pot in front of his stomach like a shield.

He likes to take the clean, empty slop buckets—where we throw leftover food—and put them over his head while cooking, which I actually find particularly hilarious. He takes the pasta pots and holds them above his stomach and then his head, chanting "potbelly, pothead" as quickly as possible, right in my face, only a few inches between our mouths, and I genuinely laugh at this, too. He makes convincing-sounding fart noises using one side of his mouth, and every time a guide enters the kitchen, he pretends that they're so flatulent he has to ask them to leave, then laughs wildly with his head thrown back, and I can't help but join in.

One morning, Sam asks me if I know how to administer CPR to an AIDS patient. When my answer is no, he shows me: he mimes stomping on a prone person's chest with one foot, and then purses his lips and blows softly downward from his upright position. The insinuation is that he's loath to touch his imaginary patient. I'm loath to be stuck in the kitchen with him at this moment. I have to laugh because he expects me to laugh, but my guts are snaky. So often, his jokes are fast and dirty and hard to keep up with, and I feel like I'm constantly being bounced around in the eddy of them.

He holds conversations with people I can't see; he leans his head forward, dipping his chin and raising his eyebrows, chuckling in commiseration or appreciation. He puts his lips to the screen of the kitchen window and whispers like he's working a drive-thru intercom. And any time I start to get disturbed by these interactions, he distracts me, singing "milk, milk, lemonade, around the corner fudge is made," pointing to his body with a pair of greasy tongs, skittering off to check on his soup on the stove.

If he stuck with his fake conversations, we'd all be fine. But he doesn't. I find that I can't listen to my headphones while working dishpit, because he has a tendency to sneak up on me and nearly hook his chin over my shoulder. He likes to talk right into my ear, his upper chest a few inches from my upper back. My only defence in these situations is laughter—I like to try to laugh as loud as he does. If I start laughing, he starts laughing, and everything is okay.

I still can't figure him out. He's a pinball, unpredictable, at one minute crooning and soothing, at the next yelling and slamming things on all the metal surfaces within his reach. Maybe his temperament is all an elaborate ruse, designed to confuse his kitchen companions. It doesn't really matter. What matters is that we all need to find our own ways to deal with him, to make our days in the dishpit palatable.

* * *

Lodge food is cyclical. Predictable. The guests eat on a seven-day schedule. Chicken, turkey, prime roast, steak, ribs, chicken, ribs: we serve the same meals all summer.

Food supply to the lodge is limited. All of the food and supplies have to be flown in by floatplane. Shipping costs about a dollar a pound—a Beaver flight is about $1,200, packed full or not—and so every shopping trip is carefully planned. Henry doesn't just send someone back in Cochrane to the grocery store; he orders directly from a supplier. Food arrives on our dock in thick white cardboard boxes. Nothing looks right. Instead of deep-green romaine hearts, northern lettuce is white, ragged shreds of watery fibre packaged in a giant plastic bag. The apples are tiny, with brown spots, and they're always

McIntosh, always tooth-cringingly tart. Every condiment is no-name, and therefore tastes a little off-putting: ketchup that's too sweet, mustard that's too strong. Besides the apples, the only other pieces of fruit we ever get are small, hard bananas that go mushy in a day, or bitter, seedy oranges.

Sometimes, we sit at the dinner table and talk about the food we miss most. We rhapsodize about asparagus, raspberries, artichokes. We try to remember what blueberries taste like as we shovel porridge into our mouths. We murmur about greens.

"Broccoli," Aubrey says around a mouthful of oats.

"Never thought I'd miss broccoli before this fucking summer," I say into my bowl.

"I'd kill someone for a peach," Syd says. There are hums of agreement around the table. Peaches, nectarines, big fat oranges. "Like, actually fucking kill a dude."

"Kale," Pete says quietly.

"Ice cream," Emma adds.

"Strawberries," Alex says with a sigh.

"Milk," I say. I drank milk by the carton at home, but I haven't seen it in weeks. We rely on cans of evaporated milk, or those tiny creamers that never have to be refrigerated. A few days ago, a group of guests brought up their own milk for coffee in the morning and left a cup of it in the fridge after they flew out. I found it before Sam could get his hands on it when I was searching for a place to put a bowl of tuna pasta salad. I turned to Robin, who was wiping a counter. We stared at each other for just a few seconds before lunging; we stood over the sink and drank from one cup in alternating gulps, gasping between each pleasurable swallow. Now I have a taste for it again, and it's driving me crazy.

Seeing food in its most voluminous denominations is disconcerting—this food is odd and large. Peanut butter arrives waxy and thick, in large plastic buckets that we need two hands to lift and move, and is spooned into reused Skippy jars in order to fool the guests into thinking we use brand names. Behind the lodge, on the dirt path, housekeepers pour canola oil from huge drums into grimy, recycled handle jugs. Meat is delivered in frozen, fatty slabs; cheese comes in heavy blocks; bread exists, wrapped in plastic, in squished boxes.

Every time the floatplanes come in with groceries—offhandedly referred to as "gross"—the girls scuttle out of our bunks. The pilots have been told to do a fly-by, which is a low buzz over the camp in order to make enough racket to wake even the sleepiest girls from their afternoon naps. Whenever I hear the familiar, dreadful bee-drone of the Beaver planes, I slither out of my bed and shove my feet into whatever shoes are closest. From all corners of camp the housekeepers run, dishevelled and bleary, down to the dock, and wait for the idling plane to putter up to us and cut its engine. The dockhands pull the packages out of the back of the plane and we help load the food into wheelbarrows. We push our loads up the precarious ramp that connects the interlock dock and the shore: not all housekeepers are good at balancing; apparently, cans of beer, when ejected from a wheelbarrow and into the shallows of the lake, float.

Sam not only has to feed the guests, he has to feed the staff, too. Our meals become reruns: Little Henrys; grilled cheese made with the plasticky orange stuff that comes in individually wrapped slices; fajitas with mystery meat; salty vegetable soup; greasy pancakes. If Sam is feeling generous, he doesn't lard on the cooking oil. If he's in a good mood, there may even be a salad. If Sam is angry, for whatever reason he's made up to create the drama of the day, he throws the grilled cheese onto the baking trays in sloppy piles. He burns the pizzas, or gives us three-day-old tuna pasta salad. Some days, he tells me I'm in charge of deciding what the rest of the staff gets to have for lunch. If I hesitate too long, or if I pick something he doesn't like or doesn't want to make, he tells me they're not going to get anything to eat at all. Even on the days when we get good lunches—tortillas, or leftover chicken made into sandwiches, or grilled cheese that isn't overdone and is piled neatly—we still remember that everything we're eating is so unhealthy it's probably doing permanent damage to our bodies.

Still, as much as we bitch, and as much as food rules our lives with an unpleasantly tight grip, the staff dining room—tiny, peeling, and shabby—is our hub. Our heartland. When we're all jammed in around the table, there isn't room to move without brushing against each other. My elbows bump into Alisa's ribcage, my forearms touch Aidan's utensils. It's up close, too close. Not close enough.

* * *

"Tiff," I plead.

She looks up from painting her nails. We have an afternoon off and all the guests are out on the lake, so we're sitting at the tables near the dock, sunning ourselves like lazy cats. Behind us, Emma and Alisa are attempting to coax the chipmunks into eating peanuts from their palms. Every few minutes, the sweet air is punctuated with their laughter. It's funny, and hearing them giggle is reassuring. Beside them, Connor is watching and taking pictures. He's trying to persuade the girls to let him trap a chipmunk in a tennis-ball can, and they're shooing him away with practised hands.

Tiff's nails are painted orange. The colour looks good in the sunlight. I squint down at her.

"Yeah?"

"Are you in the kitchen with us tonight?"

She stops, thinks, creases her brow. "Oh, yes. It's Alex's night off."

I exhale with relief.

There's something about Tiffany that calms me. Of the two head housekeepers, she gets less wound up about lodge duties than Alex, and since I run anxious, this is helpful. She has the ability to shrug off Sam's hurtful comments, to ignore Henry's drill-bit voice. It's a strategy that serves her well, and I know I can learn from her.

But there's a partition between us, one of those divisions that's created by a misplaced glance or a misfired joke and then lingers, unsaid and unaddressed, between women, feeding off of and creating insecurity. And it has the potential to fester. I don't know how to manoeuvre around it, and I don't think there's any way to lessen it, to reach over and grab her hand and pull her to me, to say *I really like you, I trust you, please also trust me.*

There's a lot about her that makes me feel like less of a woman. She wears makeup well, has beautiful long hair with ends that never seem frizzled or split. She never looks like she's at the end of her rope. Somehow, my ragged red ponytail and pale face don't measure up.

"Thank god," I say, twiddling the ends of my hair. "You're the only one who can calm him down."

There's always a head housekeeper lurking in the kitchen, unofficially working as an expediter, there to keep Sam under control—though that job can be near to impossible sometimes. Tiff, however, is better at calming Sam than Alex. She stands and snacks and talks to Sam about his family, uses her voice to soothe him like a trainer would a horse.

"He's been bad lately, huh?"

"I don't know why I piss him off so bad," I say, flicking at my nails. They're peeling from the bleach. My knuckles are dry and cracking, my cuticles torn. Before this summer, I had beautiful long nails. I shove my hands under my thighs and sit on them, hoping Tiff doesn't notice.

"Don't worry. I've been working with him for years and he still screams at me," she says, shrugging.

• • •

The problem is that Sam seems to like turmoil. He's a religious watcher of soap operas. When his wife writes to him from their home in Florida, she keeps him up to date on his shows. There's no TV signal here, so he's bereft of drama, which we're convinced is why he tries to start it within the housekeepers.

He likes to try to play us off against one another. If we come into the dishpit and the sink is already crowded with filthy pans and lids, he tells us that whoever worked the day before us left it for us, when in reality, it was him. He tells us that girl said that we were lazy, and that girl said that we didn't leave enough cleaning rags for her—because in Sam's world, we still don't seem to warrant names.

Sometimes, it goes beyond stories. One day, he makes me a batch of peanut butter Rice Krispies squares and hands them to me in front of all the other girls while we're watching a movie. "Don't share them with anyone," he says. When he walks back to the kitchen, I'm left holding the bag, flush-faced, six sets of eyes on me.

Another time, he asks me to scrub all of the lowest shelves with steel wool. My knees start to bleed as I crawl around the kitchen in order to get the job done, and the other housekeepers watch, aghast, but he doesn't let them help.

So the housekeepers create a rule: no man left behind. No woman left alone in the kitchen at the end of the night. We make sure that we all leave together. It's a hard rule to stick to when the serving and washing comes fast and thick and the sun sets so late. It's a hard rule to remember when we know there's a mickey of pilfered rum being passed around in the guide-shack as we clean and mop. But it's necessary to stay strong and true to one another. After we mop the last corner, after we dry the last knife, after we drop our aprons and trays, our power comes from leaving the kitchen as a coven, holding hands and escaping the steam, the sweat, the stink of charred meat. We debrief in groans and chuckles on the dark forest path back to our cabins, where we peel off our dirty clothes, comb out our long hair. Forget the day's bullshit. Take pleasure in knowing that we're there for one another.

● ● ●

"Two medium rare, one rare, one well done," I rattle off to Sam, shoving my notepad back down into the waistband of my pants. The paper is already damp and limp from how hard I'm sweating, and I'm sure that I have pen smudged across my lower back. Steak night is always stressful. Most of the girls hate prime roast night because it's tricky to time. Sam makes the roast early, and asking for rare or well-done slices means anxiety. Early in the evening, well done means dropping a piece of medium-rare beef into a pot of boiling water. Later in the evening, after the roast has sat, rare is an impossibility. Me, I hate steak night, when Sam stands over the grill, trying to time his cooking so that each steak is made to the guests' specifications, but all the plates have to come out together. The fans over the stove struggle to keep the intake going, and the servers smell like burned beef when we leave the kitchen.

In a way, though, we work better together when the entire kitchen staff, including Sam, is equally stressed. When he's overwhelmed, Sam has less energy to snap at us. When the servers are overwhelmed, we move around one another in well-oiled orbits, swooping full plates over each other's heads and ducking under arms heavy with accoutrements. Prima ballerinas of the tiny northern kitchen. Divas of the delicate dance. We push up our sleeves to expose Rosie the Riveter biceps, sweat collecting along our wrists and brows and making our hair stick to our napes in exquisite finger curls. We slap one another's bums to get past, shifting in and out of each other's way without thinking twice. We're comfortable with one another's bodies without being overt about it. If I were an observer, I would think us beautiful.

Busting into the kitchen, I barrel through the dishpit, where Sydney is wallowing in smoke. It coils around her head, falling across her shoulders like an extra head of hair. If it weren't such an alarming scene, it would be arresting. She looks at me, eyes narrowed. Sam has been struggling with the fans, or maybe he got a glut of orders and has thrown too many steaks on the grill. Whatever the case, the kitchen is smoking at the seams.

Without stopping my trajectory, I wink at her, clicking the side of my mouth like a cowboy.

"Stop, drop, and roll, baby," I holler. Her laughter nips at my heels as I leave the kitchen.

* * *

On one of my dishpit days, I drag myself into the kitchen. Homesickness hasn't been an issue so far, but today I feel so low. I miss my family. I miss Toronto, a comfortable mattress, a semblance of privacy. I miss having a place to shave my legs, a room in which to tell secrets. Living with so many other young men and women can be emotionally rewarding, but it's also exhausting. I'm privy to everyone's business, and they are privy to mine.

Sam is clattering around the kitchen, mumbling to himself as though he's been up for hours, despite it being 6:30 a.m. He doesn't glance over when I slide in front of the sink and tie the apron around my waist with shaking hands. The exhaustion is so deep in my bones that I can't even lift my head to look at him, to see if his body language hints at the kind of mood he's in and, therefore, what kind of day it will be.

There's a silence behind me as I start to wash the early-morning dishes—the grease-thick bacon trays, the gummy oatmeal pot. It's all I can do not to cry. I can't look forward at the expanse of the day without feeling upset.

"What's the matter with you?" His voice surprises me. He's right behind me; I didn't hear him.

If I could only tell him. I'm sad. I'm weary. I haven't had more than six hours of sleep a night since coming here. You make me anxious. I don't want to be in the kitchen today. Instead, I mutter something about missing home, my family.

Sam pauses. His energy slows down. His arms stop moving. It's rare to see him in a low phase, so I can't help but look up from my washing and stare. It's in this moment that he appears most relatable—no strange tics, no weird expressions. He's not telling jokes, not flicking his fingers at me. He's stationary, thinking. Quiet.

Then he turns and leaves. I'm left holding the oatmeal pot.

When he returns a few minutes later, he's holding a letter and some pictures. He doesn't hold them out to me at first. Instead, he leans back against the dish-drying table and looks at me, appraising. He's a different person when he's calm. He seems kindly.

"You miss them, huh?"

I nod.

"This is from my wife." Sam tentatively extends his hand. "There're photos of my grandson in there." He looks at me, as if to see if I properly value the rareness of this interaction. "He likes to make funny faces, so she took some pictures and sent 'em. I don't always like to look at them. Because they make me a little sad."

I look at the pictures of his grandson. In one photo, his little cheeks are puffed. In another, his lower lip is stuck out. I knew that Sam had a family, someone who loved him enough to write him on the regular, but seeing photographic evidence hits the point home. I look at the pictures over and over again, worried that if I give them back, I'll forget that he does have a heart, a life outside of this crummy kitchen.

I don't look up for a little while. I would never admit to having tears in my eyes, but I feel too fragile to try to commute the tenuous lines of communication that Sam and I have just strung between us. I hear him shuffle away. I'm still holding the pictures and the letters; I try to sniff quietly, so he doesn't hear me.

"Here."

I look up. He's back, holding a huge bag of cookie bars. Sam's desserts are legendary: his brownies, blondies, cookie bars, cheesecakes, crisps, and the birthday cakes he grudgingly bakes for us. Even more treasured are those peanut butter Rice Krispies squares, and his vaunted peanut butter cheesecake. Everyone pleads for extra helpings of dessert, but it rarely happens.

"I know you like 'em," he says, thrusting them at me. "So does that girl. The one who worked here yesterday."

That girl, as he calls her, has been working here for about a month. I know he knows her name. I have to smile at the absurdity of it. Maybe he doesn't want to learn our names because he knows we'll be gone next year. Some of the employees come back season after season, but many go on to pursue careers, leaving the lodge behind. He's probably seen hundreds of girls come and go. I don't believe he misses any of them, but maybe it makes him feel old, stagnant. Ossified, stuck in his tiny slap-dash kitchen, cooking on the same stovetops, making the same breakfasts.

I hold the bag of cookie bars close to my chest. Next week, Sam could make me wash all of the grill vents. I'll have to change my dishwater three times to catch even a glimpse of the steel beneath the soot and grease. I'll have to go into the pantry and cry just to make it through the day, and I'll have to run back into the kitchen when I hear him howling for me through the thin walls. This moment won't change anything. But for now, I won't think about that. I only know that the cookie bars are still warm against my skin, and that I feel better.

TROUBLE BEAR

On a late June afternoon, one of those days when the air is so heavy that the camp falls quiet under its dozy blanket, Henry strides into the main building, where I'm working floater duties, and asks if I want to see a bear up close. The beauty and the downside of having a dump near the lodge is that it attracts a group of black bears that grow more accustomed to humans than is proper; dump bears don't have to scavenge for food, because they have a rotting buffet at their disposal. Murphy, who's a hunting guide when he's not at Kesagami, warned me that it was going to be an active summer for bears, since he saw so many of them from the plane on the flight up. We've been dealing with the bears on and off in a peripheral way—the dockhands have gotten especially used to seeing curious eyes in the forest, and we've found a few garbage cans knocked over some mornings.

Some of the other workers have seen bears this summer, but I haven't. I'm sure at any given time I've been within a dozen or so feet of one without noticing; being in the vicinity of a bear seems unavoidable. Putting yourself close to one on purpose is, to me, incredibly foolish. But anything is better than sitting alone at the bar, washing Thermoses. Henry has worked us so hard and this seems like a truce. His eyes are lit up in a boyish way, and I sense that there's no ulterior motive. I want to see what my boss is like when he's truly enjoying this place. And I want to go home having seen a bear.

I've never been to the dump. The housekeepers have motioned to it during our "cleaning the forest" chores, which is when Henry asks us to move branches he thinks are unsightly from the underbrush so the fishermen can't see them when they walk the paths. *That back there is the dump, don't really need to go there, really only a place the boys go when they do the burn, lots of bears there.* Those are the sentiments about the dump, which exists back in the spruce, back down along the path Henry stands on, grinning. It's exceptionally unsettling to be staring down the throat of the forest, but I figure I'm safe with him, probably, and there's no better time than the present to see the guts of the place. So far, I've managed to pretend that I'm not really as far north as I am. I've stuck to the paths that connect the cabins, the well-trod shoreline, the bunks and bathrooms. And now, I know, is the time for the baptism by fully immersing myself in the green that spreads, silent and waiting.

I follow Henry dutifully along the path, trying to keep my breathing even. With every step I take, I'm surprised at how far I feel from the lodge. The farther back we go, foot by foot, the quieter it gets, and the more the noise from the activity at Kesagami is intensely and rapidly muffled. Even though Henry is only a few feet ahead of me, it feels as if no one else exists; the spruce trees are so thick that I feel alone, as if I've gone back in history. And the forest is painfully green: moss on the tree trunks, needles on the dry ground, the brush crackling underfoot. The smell of it surrounds me, forcing its way into me. This isn't the forest in a fairytale where girls befriend the beasts they find. This is real.

Henry walks confidently in front; I follow a few paces behind, out of deference, and also defence—I figure that if a bear lunges, he'll be between me and its claws and teeth. I'm a bit appalled at myself for imagining my boss as bear bait, but as we get further into the summer, my thinking has gotten starker and starker. He's talking about the dinner service, the new guests flying into camp, the current state of the dump and how that bodes for forest-fire prevention. I tune him out, and focus on the *one-two-one-two* of our combined footsteps on the soft soil. I can see only his heels in my up-eye vision. And then—

"There he is," Henry says, and I can hear his smile without seeing his face.

The bear is a big boy, well over two hundred pounds, with a white blaze across his broad chest. We're about twenty feet away, so he hasn't deemed us a threat. Or maybe we haven't entered his scent stream. He's nosing around in the garbage, whuffling from pile to pile, his big rump wobbling as he shifts back and forth. I can hear his exhalations, breathy wheezes and fluttering sighs, as if he's demarcating his triumphs and frustrations. I'm surprised: he looks funny, even harmless. But that doesn't stop my pulse from drumming against my throat and through the cage of my breastbone. I try to breathe quietly through my nose, and I keep my mouth closed for fear of gasping. Henry crouches, and I follow suit. We shuffle forward, my heart whumping in my chest. Can the bear hear us? Can he smell us?

Despite having what looks like a cumbersome body, black bears are remarkably expressive, almost elegant in how they communicate using their physicality. I watch this bear assess his situation and environment through his senses, and I'm amazed. He has a demonstrative face: eyebrows that furrow or rise, eyes that narrow or widen. His ears are perked; he's listening. His nose wiggles seemingly independently of the rest of his body as he tastes the air. He bends, dips his head, and uses the tips of his claws to ease open the plastic wrap on a half-eaten sandwich. He *unwraps* it.

Henry looks back at my surprised face and smiles. "Ask the housekeepers about the time a bear unlatched the walk-in fridge and ate all of the sandwiches from the packed lunches," he whispers. "They were covered in cling wrap. He got 'em out."

Suddenly, the bear stops nosing. His head swivels, his structure moving with incredible, frightening grace, as he spots us. He raises up, his body moving in segments like some kind of machine. First his ears prick up, then his face rises, then his chest broadens, and then he's entirely up on his hind legs, his paws close to his chest. My heart gallops, and my vision silvers over as he turns his full attention to us. He moves his spine eerily, shifting the upper part of his body out to one side to see us better while keeping his hind legs planted on the ground and motionless. He readies himself. He stares us down.

I've never felt fear like this. It's vestigial, instinctual, power-ful; it pulses through me with every panicked beat of my heart. It's all I can do to focus on breathing, on not running away. The bear looks at me and we stand, locked in the moment.

*　　*　　*

My fascination with black bears comes from my deep, meaty fear of them. When I was deciding to take this job, the idea of working in close proximity to these bears was a huge red tick in the nega-tives column, something filed under "this scares the shit out of me," even more than having to make friends with other young women, even more than spending weeks in close quarters with young men. The spectre of the bear—in my lurid nightmares tall and slavering, towering over a fragile human body with teeth bared and claws out—made my stomach knot up in a jagged way. The fear comes from the same place inside of me where other unadulterated emotions—lust, hunger, frustration—are born and bred. So I tried to learn. I spent hours down the Google rabbit hole; I pulled papers from the UBC library website. Even now I find a battered book in the lodge's book collection—a sad shelf, mostly full of incongruous romance novels with pulpy covers and titles like *Rangoon* and *This Fiery Splendor* that we giggle over while on break—that I fish out and read covertly in my bunk, late at night, when the others are painting their toenails or brushing the snarls out of their hair.

I might be scared of them, but the consensus is that bears are fascinating, powerful animals, one of those species that has cap-tured human interest and held that interest for millenniums.

Black bears are the only type of bear found exclusively in North America; Canada has three species of bears—black, brown (with its intimidating grizzly subspecies), and the ever scary polar. There aren't any grizzlies in Ontario, and we're too far south for polar bears (although Cochrane has a polar bear habitat for hapless tourists and a giant replica of a polar bear looming over the information centre). We're smack in the middle of black bear territory; we're summer neighbours with these spirits.

A black bear weighs about the same as an average human male, somewhere between 160 and 220 pounds, although a good-sized black bear can reach anywhere upward of 250 pounds, with some big old boys reaching 500 pounds; the biggest black bear documented in Ontario weighed 760 pounds and was more than six feet long. Despite their brawn, black bears are disarming because of their appearance: they have a droopy backside and wiggle when they walk because they're pigeon-toed; they move in a strange lope. Their claws are shorter than grizzly bears' claws, which means they're much more adept at climbing, but they look funny when they shimmy up tree trunks in a bunching, inchworm movement. I like what I read in the creaky old book I've swiped from the lodge library, where the authors tell me that "the bear is like a macho bullfighter whose grace and precision seem to contradict his somewhat portly appearance."

And bears are greedy for food and for knowledge, always hungry and always, always curious, so curious that they get themselves into jams. There's a 1976 article from an Alberta newspaper that describes an incident in which a motorist foolishly stopped by the side of the road on the Banff-to-Jasper highway to get a closer look at a black bear. While he did this, the curious bear moseyed around to the other side of the car, slipped into the driver's seat, and accidentally nudged the gear-shift with its body. The car rolled off the road; the bear made a terrified exit, and the car owner an equally terrified re-entrance and getaway.

But they're far from just clowns. They're the ancient care-takers of this land. It's easy for us to imagine ourselves invin-cible, since there's never been a bear-related incident at the lodge, but we're not. They're the gods. The bears have seen hundreds of us come and go; they've watched quiet and blink-ing from their bear paths hidden beyond the lines of the forest. We're working near important and intimidating animals that know the land better than we do and tolerate us regardless. We're living among one of the world's most prolific and mis-understood predators, an animal that has been documented and revered for ages.

Looking at a bear, it's easy to understand why they were wor-shipped; they are like us, but not us. Bears walk plantigrade— with their full weight on the soles of the feet, not on fingers or claws—the same way humans do. They can stand on their hind legs and sometimes even walk upright; they reach and grab with almost the same mannerisms as us; a bear skeleton is said to look like a human skeleton. This could be why bears scare humans so much, why we talk about them so often. As the book in my hands says: "We cannot shake off the impression that behind the long muzzle and beneath the furry coat so unlike our naked skin there is a self not so different from us."

*   *   *

My fear of bears hasn't decreased now that I've seen one. I think it's increased, despite the fact that nothing grievous happened at the dump; the bear we were peering at just ignored us and went back to eating garbage. Now I've seen, in person, how those animals move—the sheer, luscious muscularity married with devastating grace. Now I know for certain that they're the top predators on this land, that we would be nothing in the face of an attack if it were to happen. Now I know that they're meant to be feared and revered, all in one emotional package.

I'm alone in this feeling; the other staff members mostly wave off my bear concerns.

"Good lord, Big Rig. Get a grip!"

"There's worse to worry about up here. Like how you're going to serve that annoying party of drunks tonight for dinner."

"They're just big dummies."

"We have bear-bangers. Don't worry."

"Man, I hunted one with a broken wine bottle once."

An average of fewer than one person a year is killed by black bears across all of North America. And when black bears do kill people, it seems to be either for necessity—feeding on the body—or because they've never seen a human before and are taken aback. But sometimes there's no reason or rhyme to fatal bear attacks: you can do everything right and still fall prey. You can have food in the campfire frying pan and still become dinner. Some things are out of our control.

Because we're so far north, and it's hard for representatives from the Ministry of Natural Resources to get to us in a timely manner, the MNR has given us permission to kill what are deemed "nuisance bears." *Nuisance* sounds light-hearted: it would be more prudent to call it a *trouble* bear, an *angry* bear, a bear with a brain in which wires have become crossed. Under normal circumstances, when ministry representatives can get to a site quickly, a representative visits and assesses what attracted the bear in the first place. There's a chain of events and red tape and all efforts are taken to keep the public and the bears safe. All of this is fair and valid and important. But up here, where MNR reps can only come in on choppy, preplanned plane rides, we don't have the luxury of time or space. So instead we're renegades, operating on our own schedule and land-based laws.

From what I've heard, it seems that a nuisance bear is killed every summer. Henry has his faults, but he's discerning when it comes to preservation and wildlife, and I trust him when it comes to deciding which bears are safe and which ones aren't. Throw in Murphy, who makes a living off of hunting, and Pea and Jack, who have seen many bears over the years, and I feel we have a good tribunal. When a bear *is* killed, its body is taken via boat to one of the islands and left there to decompose. Some of the fishing guests have dubbed this area of the lake Stinky Bay, because of the perpetual smell of decomp. A year or so later, only the skeleton remains. Sometimes, the bear bones are scooped up by guests or guides, and some have been brought back to the lodge. For years, the skulls were kept on the ground by the path leading to the dump, until a group of Cree elders visited and told Henry that keeping bear skulls on the ground was disrespectful and that they needed to be elevated. Now the skulls are nailed to the trees, right where one of the well-worn bear paths intersects with the path to the dump.

* * *

For some reason, I thought that after I saw a bear, up close and personal, something would change. But nothing did because of course that's the way it goes. Our bears ignore us, or do what they want to do without paying much attention. Winnie-the-Pooh was, after all, a black bear, I remind myself. The image is not far off; whenever a housekeeper comes across a bear—on the other side of the laundry field, across the dump, back behind the woodpile at the rear of the lodge—the bear usually toddles off after an exchange of surprised stares from both sides. It's as if we can hear them sighing—*these idiots again.* It's a fair reaction; we've expanded into their territory. It's believed that black bears need up to forty square kilometres of land to live on, if the land is rich and prolific; if not, the bear might need up to one hundred square kilometres. This means we're in their house. We're their guests. We're not good guests, either, but the bears don't get violent with us.

They do, however, let us know when we're irritating them. A little female yearling attaches to the housekeepers and becomes a common fixture around the lodge. One night, she methodically knocks over every single trash can in camp and nothing else. A few days later, the same young bear runs through the laundry field after Sydney has finished hanging all of the guest linens and pulls down every single bedsheet, leaving them in a tangled, dirty pile on the grass. "Come on, man," Syd yells when she discovers the carnage, but she starts to laugh, because how can you not?

In Sweden, tradition holds that anyone who encounters a

bear at close range need only say, "Bear, you are not baptized from the same font as I am!" and the bear can be expected to then run away in heathen embarrassment. I don't know about Swedish bears, but I have serious doubts about the effectiveness of this method. Our bobbling, persistent Ontario dump bears seem determined to continue about their daily business regardless of anything we say or do.

A joke starts in the back girls cabin over whether we should leave our window open at night.

"Why wouldn't we?" Syd asks.

"Because of bears," I say, gesturing to the window like a madwoman.

Our cabin's one operational window is a wide swath of chest-level screen that's covered only by a piece of mouldy plywood held in place with a crude latch. The only way to get a cross-breeze is to unlatch the wood and let it swing open, but when we do this we have no privacy whatsoever because the open window looks right out onto the back path. If a bear were truly curious, it could open up our cabin like a tin of sardines.

"Do you think a bear," Syd starts, laughing and barely able to get the words out, "is going to punch through the screen—like this?" She mimics a bear, throwing her head back and making a strangled roar. I can't help myself; I laugh with the rest of the girls. When she puts it like that, the whole scenario seems ridiculous. So we decide to leave the window open at night, but I know, deep in my gut, that the bears peep in on us, pressing their noses to the screen and sniffing at the flavour of our dreams, and I'm not sure if this scares or reassures me.

* * *

A week later—just after Canada Day when we're all still thinking about the festive red-and-white cake Sam made as a special
treat—our hand is forced and the truce is torn up. We have to
make a decision about the fate of one of the camp bears. A large
male with a red patch of hair on his head starts stalking the
housekeepers in the laundry field. He starts hanging around
the back girls cabin, watching. Henry has a serious look on his
face when he tells me this. I know he doesn't particularly want
to kill the bear, although I wonder if a small part of him, something to do with a sense of masculinity and proprietorship,
wants to get the adrenaline flowing, wants to pull the trigger.

I'm on bar duty; it's that lull in the day after guests have
come off the lake, and the lodge is quiet as fishermen shower
and get ready to eat dinner. Henry's not around, so some of
the more brazen dockhands and guides are sitting by one of the
fireplaces, warming their hands and feet after a long day on
the water. The main building has a beautiful glow to it as the
sun dips in the sky, which only serves to illuminate the boys'
faces. They're cracking their necks, fidgeting with their bibs
and knee-high rubber boots, running their hands through their
hat-tousled hair. They surround me. They rest their elbows
on the bar as I try to clean the Thermoses and lunchboxes from
the day. They interrupt my work with the ease of makeshift
brothers. I don't shoo them away. There's something comforting about having them around—they make me feel less lonely.
They smell like lake and outdoors, and it reminds me of what's
beyond the lodge door.

Sam waltzes out of the kitchen with a plate of muffins. He bakes them fresh and oily throughout the day; he keeps them on the hood of the stove, or balances a plate on the fingertips of one hand and doles them out to the male staff members who pass through his kitchen. Sometimes, if the housekeepers are feeling cocky, we steal a muffin every time we slither by the stovetop, but only if we're close to completely sure that Sam's napping in his bunk. He never, ever gives his muffins to the girls.

The boys lurch forward from where they've been huddled around the fireplace. They grab the baking with their dirty hands. Sam grins at me and turns away, retreating back to his kitchen kingdom with the empty plate. I sag a little, hungry for dinner, exhausted by the thought that I haven't won Sam over, not even after our strange détente. Things have gone right back to where they were before. I watch as the majority of the boys stuff muffins in their faces, talking around the carrot and cinnamon, spraying crumbs onto one another.

Jack slings his torso onto the bar beside me. He's talking over his shoulder to Kev about the bear. Without looking at me, without sliding any pity my way, he breaks his little muffin in half. Steam curlicues out and into the space between us. He hands me my portion and then retreats without making eye contact, without ever even having stopped chatting. My heart splits open like it's been peeled. I pop the muffin in my mouth before Sam can come out and see me, and feel a swell of tenderness. Then I listen in to see if I can glean any more information about our bear.

Jack and Kev are reminiscing about how one year the dockhands had to crawl belly-down through the underbrush of the forest, armed only with rake handles and glass bottles, advancing on a bear that had been shot and injured. They wanted to make sure it was good and dead, and it became play-war, exciting. They crept toward it, shooting bangers and howling wildly, a makeshift guerrilla force.

"Shoot a bear dead on," Jack says, nodding sagely, "and it's useless. Their skulls are so thick it won't kill 'em. I seen a guy shoot three times at a black bear and the bullets only just furrowed through the skin, up the ridge of the skull." He motions with his fingers, and I feel queasy, the muffin turning over in my stomach. "Gotta get it in the jaw."

"Oh."

"You know Hank wants to do it tonight, so it doesn't get you when you leave?" Jack asks, assessing me.

"What?"

"Yeah, man," Jack says.

I swallow drily. The guides have noticed it prowling around the other women, only the women for some reason, but not me. I haven't met this trouble bear. Now I feel like I'm responsible for his impending death.

"I'm gonna help," Jack continues, finally eating his half of the muffin. I brace myself on the bar, tuck some hair behind my ear. I don't want to be privy to this, and I don't want to hear how bears died in previous years. Jack grins, excited for the chase.

● ● ●

Later, only one shot sounds—clear, deep, thick. The noise bounces off of the trees and ricochets through the doorway of the lodge, falling dully to the bottom of my gut.

When Henry asks me if I want to see the dead bear, I go out of duty. The other housekeepers are already posing for pictures with it. It's piled into one of our rusty wheelbarrows. It shit itself in its moment of death. Henry nailed it in the jaw, and part of its face has blown away, its jowls covered with gelatinous red blood. I stand beside the wheelbarrow. I don't want to look down at it. Instead, I stare up at the trees as I burrow one hand into its thick fur, which is coarser than I imagined. Strong-smelling, like musk and fear and wisdom. I dig my fingers in, touching the still-warm body underneath the hide, and wonder why I feel close to crying.

BEYOND THE VEIL

Usually, when Wade comes into the staff dining room, we all chant "Wade, Wade-Wade-Wade, Wade-Wade-Wade, Wade-Wade-Waaaaaaaaaaaaaaade," to the tune of "Eye of the Tiger," a practice that Jack started on a particularly cabin-fevery morning. Wade typically graces us with a small smile and shakes his head, as if he's trying to switch us off and distract us from our embarrassing show of giddiness; he'll grab a spoon and the oatmeal ladle, and plunk down next to one of the guys at the far end of the table. But our song peters out as we realize, one by one, that something is wrong today. Wade looks off; he seems distracted, clammy and pale.

"What's wrong, man?" Aidan presses him.

Wade shakes his head. "I don't—" That's when we all study him, because if Wade, strong Wade, doesn't want to talk about something, it could be something bad.

"Spit it out," Jack barks, a forkful of eggs halfway to his mouth.

Wade shifts his jaw, and I can hear his teeth creak. He doesn't want to speak about it, but he's so sleep-deprived that his better judgment takes a back seat, and he starts talking. He tells us that he woke up damp and confused last night, needing to take a piss. It was about 3 a.m., he says. Hot as hell, the air thick, the moon a weak scrap. He was too lazy to walk to the bathhouse to use the urinals, so he opened the door of the cabin and decided to relieve himself against the outdoor wall. Nothing really out of the ordinary there, I think. Even the women do this on some nights, if we're too sleepy to walk to the motel bathrooms, though it's a little more precarious for us to piss against a wall in the dark.

"Okay, whatever," Connor says, shoving a piece of bread in his mouth and chasing it with a slug of weak coffee.

"Yeah, but in the middle of it, I looked up and there was a fucking . . . a fucking wolf, man," Wade stutters.

A week or so ago, during the lull before dinner, when the housekeepers were waiting around in the dining room, a tipsy guest showed me some pictures he took a few years ago, photos of a huge, white animal. I assessed the parts I understood: thick fur, a canine head held at an insouciant angle, lantern eyes flicking back over a shoulder to cast a disinterested look at the annoying mammals gawking from the boat. There were only a few shots, the guest told me as I thumbed through his pride-and-glory photos, because *he disappeared so damn quickly.*

I smiled to be polite, and handed the photos back. The truth is, the men up here are always trying to impress the house-keepers with something. *I got bit by a pike, didn't even wince; I saw a bear swimming alongside our boat and tried to touch him; I got a fishing lure stuck in my cheek when I tried to cast; I fell into the water drunk and only just got missed by the motor.*

Every single day, we have to resist rolling our eyes at some form of long-cocking, some tall tale, some harebrained excuse to talk to us and slow down our chores. This story, those photos— they both might fall into that category. None of us has actually seen a wolf, so we don't think about them too much. We're more concerned with the creatures that seek us out on purpose, like bears, like blackflies.

"Go on! Get outta town!" As if Wade's turning into one of those guests, telling a tall tale to freak us out. We're into July now. We've sweated out our naïveté; we're more hardened, like our legs and biceps have become from the weeks of work. This must be a mirage, caused by the hazy late days of summer.

Wade shakes his head. "No, I'm telling you," he says, putting his face in his hands for a moment. We laugh uneasily as he rubs his eyes with his thumbs. "I'm telling you . . ."

And then he tells us the real story, the real reason that his eyes are ringed with dark circles and his voice is hoarse. I listen, gob open, as he tells us that he dropped his hands and stopped his piss midway through. That he moved away as slowly as he could, and fell backward into the cabin. Slammed the door behind him. That after he locked his door, he heard what sounded like fingernails dragging along the wood of the cabin. Heard what he thought was human sobbing from the other side of the door, even though he was sure that he was alone, that he was the only one awake in the entire camp. Even though it wasn't a human he saw.

Wade looks up, his eyes bleary. "It was fucked, man."

Pranks and ghost stories are currency. Someone is always trying to scare someone else, whether it's a dockhand locking a housekeeper in the laundry room, or a housekeeper hiding under the covers in a fishing guide's bunk. Gus, the housekeepers tell me, has the *best* ghost stories out of all the staff members; when I ask him, however, he refuses to spill. "You'll get too scared," he says without smiling. I let the subject drop because there's something about his tone that warns me off. Later, the guides and dockhands tell me that Gus was just trying to freak me out, and I try to laugh the whole interaction off, not quite convinced.

But this doesn't seem like a prank.

"Shit—"

There's nothing to say, no more jokes to be made. This is something we haven't yet experienced. The otherworldly has mostly left us alone, despite the ghost stories, burial grounds, things that happened in the past in the motel, which the veteran girls swear is haunted. We've managed to skirt most of the spirits we've heard talk about. But maybe not anymore.

"It was fucked," he repeats, his head in his hands.

* * *

Before I came to this place, I had never heard silence and symphony at the same time. Now I can hear a thick vein of quiet that throbs below the day and night life. The nights sound like nothing and a thousand things at once, a cacophony: wings and chitin, tongues on fur, clacking of keratin, thrums from the tree branches and the huge platter of the water. There's also the hum of the fishing lodge's generator, the burble of drunken fishermen. And underneath it all—or on top of it all, maybe—there's something else, something patient, silent, something that exists beyond the reach of my words. During the day, we fill the air with our whoops and shrieks and stupid hollers. We thrive in the light, pretending we're the kings and queens of the castle. But once the sun sets, the balance of power shifts. When the day fades into indigo, when the darkness crawls in from sky and shoreline, toward our cabins, something changes.

When darkness falls, the land's psychology shifts; there's an undertone of quiet menace. In the dark, we can't see more than a few feet ahead of us, don't know what's waiting for us at the edge of the forest or farther down the paths. In the dark, we go to sleep, useless to do much else. And in the dark, other beings wake up, stretch, speak, and fill the night with their sounds.

But there's one sound I've been waiting to hear. It's the sound that tears out of that mysterious animal that lives cloaked, slinky and secretive, and captivates my imagination like no other. It's the sound of calling out to a clan.

The wolf is an interesting study in contrasts. They're not as large and therefore not as visually intimidating as bears—in the taiga, the timber wolf can weigh anywhere from 66 to 154 pounds—but they're prolific predators nonetheless. Timber wolves travel in packs of a dozen or fewer, and these large numbers allow them to target and take down big prey, the big mammals: caribou, moose. They also kill their canine relatives, coyotes and foxes, without remorse. And their territory is large: wolves in Ontario can live on anywhere from 1,000 to 1,100 square kilometres of land.

So it seems cocky, I know, to think that of all the acreage a wolf could choose from, it would choose our lodge and our forests, would decide to be our neighbour for the summer. Would let us see it, hear it. Before coming up here, I'd imagined glamorous, mournful sounds on the wind that I would be able to turn into boastful memories later. I figured I'd be able to step outside of a cabin and cock my head and listen for that famous sound. But so far, nothing. It's as if the North is teasing me: *You want this? It's not going to happen. You thought you'd get something? Not a chance.*

There's such a widely held fascination with wolves, maybe even more than with bears or eagles or fish. You can see it in the way people try to align themselves with lupines: humans wear lurid illustrations of howling wolves on T-shirts, maybe ironically, maybe not; gift shops across the country are filled with wolf trinkets like jewellery, magnets, shot glasses, beach towels; if we're "running with the wolves" or "howling at the moon," we're exploring wild archetypes. It seems as if the big bad wolf has been transformed into something of an idol instead of a villain. In fact, I'm asked about wolves three times as much as I'm asked about any other local animal; guests are drawn to the idea of them. A big part of it must be that wolves look like dogs, that they have that pearlescent, thousand-yard stare and the aloofness that holds them apart and perhaps above other animals, but still resemble man's best friend. And it must be because wolves, too, have so much mythology hitched to them: the wolf was said to be sacred to the god Apollo; Norse mythology holds that Skoll and Hati, two wolves, chased the sun and the moon across the sky; that the giant wolf Fenrir, son of Loki, had a mouth that was so big that when he opened it, one jaw touched heaven and one touched the earth.

And then there's that howling.

It's a popular sound effect used in movies and on Halloween tapes; we've all heard a variant of it. That howl stokes odd gut reactions: it fascinates, frightens, makes our hair stand up in a way that's pleasurable, unpleasant, and satisfying all at once. A wolf's howl is said to travel distances of fifteen kilometres or more; it teases, never betraying its hidden owner, and that makes us antsy, melancholy. It says *where are you, where are you*, and then the answer comes, broken and hitched in the most beautiful way: *I'm here, I'm here*—a dialogue that prickles at the base of our brain. Loneliness, uncertainty, eeriness: the howl brings all of those feelings out. Mournful and eddying, it dances on the edge between our everyday world and a world that exists beyond the veil.

There's something nameless that exists up here, something with strength and tenacity, something tied to the land and the lake. It's always present. I feel it when I walk the back pathway, when I take a few steps into the thicket of spruce and I'm clasped by silence. I feel it in the urge to lock the cabin door at night, in my reluctance to go swimming in the lake on my own. It's not necessarily a danger, because there are real threats. Instead, the feeling is like a pressure: a force that is always present but not always insistent. It might be said that there's an *electricity* to the land, that it's all about being pinned in between some magical longitude and latitude, but that's not quite right; it's too easy of a solution and too tired of a trope.

Some of the staff members are blithe about this presence to the point of intentional disrespect. They hike far back into the bush, hacking down trees for firewood, complaining about the bugs and the heat and the work and the land. *Fuck this*, they snarl. *Hate this place.*

Some of us are wary. We refuse to travel into the forest by ourselves, demand a buddy system for hanging the linens in the isolated laundry field. We link arms when we have to slip into the woods to travel to the dump. We sing when we walk alone on the paths, raising our voices to the canopy and refusing to look up or to the side or anywhere we might see something staring back at us.

And some of us have silent reverence. We tip our heads to the crows, mumbling reassurances so softly that no one else can hear us and make fun. We steal cigarettes from the guest rooms and burn them as offerings while out on the lake in a canoe, looking to see if there are eyes somewhere deep in the trees.

●　●　●

Kesagami Lake has many islands: there's Big Island, which is close to the lodge; Manidoo Island, with a spit of sand reaching out into the lake and an eagles' nest in a tree near the shoreline; Fossil Island, where there's an active Indigenous burial ground and where no boat is to dock, ever. And then there's Windigo Island, which we're not to point at, because it supposedly brings bad weather. I've heard stories that, many years ago, a local woman was left there to die, but, like many of the stories at Kesagami, that could be hearsay.

Windigo has many names: Weetigo, Weeghtako, Wehtigo, Weendigo, Witiko, Whit te co—there are dozens of ways to spell it, and all of them imbue the same fear in those who know it: the

man-eater. I can't know Windigo; it's not my heritage and therefore it's not my spirit. I don't have the right or intellect to fully
put it into words. Windigo comes from Algonquian culture, a
grouping that is composed of peoples who speak the Algonquian
languages. This includes, but is not limited to: Ojibwe/Chippewa;
a variety of Cree groups; Algonkin; Mi'kmaq; Naskapi; and possibly the Beothuk people of Newfoundland.

Nowadays, Windigo has become a thing of pop culture. It's
been turned into a whitewashed, grotesque bogeyman in
shows like *Supernatural* and *Charmed*; it's been made into
the villain of video games and is a creature in *Dungeons &
Dragons*, where it's described as "a strange, savage fey spirit";
people think it's appropriate to cosplay as Windigo at comic
cons. In 1973, Windigo even fought the Incredible Hulk and
Wolverine in a Marvel comic book. In my undergrad psychology textbooks, Windigo psychosis is explained as a "dramatic" mental illness in which people have a craving to eat
human flesh.

In an unofficial-looking comb-bound stack of papers called
Windigo: An Anthology of Fact and Fantastic Fiction that I find
wedged into a library shelf, nearly all the writing seems to be by
white men. According to this publication, in 1636, Father Paul
Le Jeune, a Jesuit missionary living and working in French
Canada, wrote to his superiors about a "Demon" who ate some
"Tribes that live north of the River which is called the tree
Rivers." Le Jeune uses the term "Atchen," but this still may be
the first written reference to Windigo from a settler—Windigo
as a werewolf-like figure terrorizing the Attikamegouekhin people. The earliest English documentation of the word *Windigo*

comes from James Isham, in 1743. Isham was a trader for the Hudson's Bay Company, and interacted with the Cree people who came to trade at York Factory on the west coast of Hudson Bay.

"Whit te co," he writes. "The devil."

So I've been exposed to Windigo as settlers have imagined it—brawny and brash, pulpy and popular, as an undiscerning monster that tears people from tip to tail—but in order to learn about Windigo, truly, without the colonial gloss, there's deeper digging to do. It's easy to find writing from white people on Windigo; settlers have always had better access to platforms on which to share their points of view. It's harder to find Indigenous writers who have been vaunted the same way, who have been afforded the same opportunities. This is the paradox of researching Windigo: the main information I'm able to find isn't the information I really want or value.

Here's what I can glean: Windigo is a cannibal. Windigo is a demon that stalks the boreal woods at night. Windigo has a taste for human flesh, feeds on it. It's both a thing of myth and a reality, as seen in the documented cases of people "becoming" Windigo and eating—or wanting to eat—human flesh. Windigo is a personification of spiritual and physical famine. Basil Johnston, Anishinaabe scholar, believes that the term *Weendigo* may come from Ojibway words: *ween dagoh* ("solely for self") or *weenin n'd'igooh* ("fat," "excess"). Other sources say that the name comes from the Cree word *wihtikowiw* ("she or he eats greedily").

I can't help but think of Windigo when I look out to that island, when nighttime falls and the camp changes. It's easy to pin all fears on one figure—a ghost, a demon, something that becomes a scapegoat. Human beings think we want to know what is staring back from the unfathomable darkness of the depthless woods. We think we already know what it might be, based on settler "knowledge."

But who is carving the logging roads through the green velvet of the forest around Cochrane? Who is trawling the lake for its biggest fish? Who is trapping the groundhogs, chasing away the bears, pestering and attempting to get photos of the wolves and the moose? Who is trying so stubbornly to keep a fishing lodge running in an environment that is clearly inhospitable? Windigo is not just one thing; there are many, many Windigos. We—the settlers who think we know about this land, we use it and abuse it and like to forget that it's not ours and never will be—are not as good as we think we are.

Windigo is as tall as the pine trees it stalks through. Windigo is everybody. Windigo is naked and lanky; it's impervious to the boreal cold. Windigo is your neighbour. Windigo is so powerful and swift that it can stride across a lake, and nobody can outrun it. Windigo is my cabinmate, my co-worker, my boss. Windigo has a black hole of a mouth, lips eaten away from its own hunger, hollow, dark holes for eyes. Windigo has red hair and wears a green shirt. Windigo is always hungry, always searching. Windigo wants more.

●　●　●

One night, I wake up with a full bladder. So far, I've avoided this situation by being prudent about water consumed before bed. Nobody wants to have to wriggle out of a sleeping bag and tumble out of a cabin into the witching hour. But this need is insistent. It won't go away, even when I turn from side to side, crossing my legs at the ankles. Beside me, my three cabin-mates loll, soundless, far into the pleasures of sleep.

There's a choice to be made. Do I walk through a portion of the woods to get to the flushing toilets? Or do I prop myself against the cabin and let it rip? The toilet paper and running water sound great, but I'm not brave enough to shine my flashlight into the dark. I tell myself that it's because of the bears; that I'm too tired to walk that far; that this is easier. And then I unlatch the cabin door.

I know Kesagami well enough at dusk, when I admire the sunsets before I flitter into my cabin and lock the door. But this, the lodge in the middle of the deep night, is different. It feels and looks as though I've stepped onto another planet. I even move slower than I normally would. My feet don't make a sound on the forest floor and my skin stays silent when my legs rub against each other with every step. Above me, the moon is green, the stars shining a strange lime, and it feels as if the light and the foliage and the warm, moist breath of the nighttime wind are all interacting with one another in that symphony. The trees are using the motionless night to react and extend and glow. The leaves are still, yet somehow also rustle in the breeze—an exhalation, a sigh at having been disturbed by my opening the door.

I hold my hands out, stupefied. My palms are nacreous in the lodge floodlights, but there isn't the shadow of a single nocturnal moth along my lifelines, no other movement anywhere. The throbbing quiet clings to me when I pull my underwear down.

When I lean against the cobwebbed cabin wall, I'm so scared. I think about ghosts. I think about that wolf patrolling the hem of the forest. I think about all of the things I don't know about the land I'm trying to live on. I keep my eyes closed the entire time and pray that I'm good enough to be passed over.

It turns out that it's too stressful to keep negotiating with the land; it's a losing battle. So I lay rules out in my head: no more pissing outside the cabins at night; no more lazily flinging broken branches into the forest's cusp instead of properly burning them for firewood; no more calling the animals names behind their backs. The land isn't changing for us, something I should have realized by now. I should be changing myself for the land—at least for these last few weeks.

When the sun sets late on a nastily hot day, the housekeepers leave our clothes on the shore and breaststroke into the amber light, dipping below the surface and letting the water turn us beautiful again. When the entire camp, guests included, is rain-lashed into a ground-bound rain day, we pin up a makeshift tarpaulin shelter, light a fire, and learn to make bannock from some of our Cree guests. We nod to the bears; we stop pestering the pike. We work. We buckle down. We dig, we haul, we chop, we lug, we transfer dirt and rocks from one side of the shore to the other, but we do it all knowing that our efforts are never going to stick, that we're a temporary mark on the land. And we become okay with that. We learn to value ourselves just a little bit less, revere the land just a little bit more.

We learn to laugh at ourselves, even in the face of fear. One night, a few days after Wade's story, enough time that we have started to forget it, the four of us return to the back cabin sweaty and tired. We've taken to walking outside in groups, talking and making noise. Some of us have even started singing 1980s songs like "Eye of the Tiger" and Tommy Tutone's "867-5309/ Jenny" as loud as we can, to try to lessen the intensity of the quiet woods.

We slink through our front door, trying to get the nightly dinner menu out of our heads. Now is the time for shucking serving whites and slipping into well-worn sweatpants and sandals. I stretch the muscles of my feet on the bench by our front door as Robin starts to undo her braids, closing her eyes as she digs her fingertips into her scalp. At the end of the night, we can smell one another's sweat, meat grease from the grill, soap and bleach from the dishpit. But it doesn't matter; we still lean into one another with exhaustion. Syd reaches up and turns on the overhead light. The cabin lights up, and all of a sudden, I see a hand sticking out from under Syd's bunk. The hand is holding a hamburger bun.

Before I have time to get scared, to wonder why a dismembered ghost hand is holding a hunk of bread, Gus erupts from under the bed. He stands up to his full height, howling as loud as he can, arms outstretched like branches.

We all scream at the absolute top of our lungs. We jump into one another, grabbing at arms and legs and shoulders and whatever meat we can get our hands on. My heart contracts and expands in a quick rhythm, and Syd and I bury our faces in each other's necks, breathing in the scent of familiar female. I know it's just Gus, because I can see his giant grin through the fragile fence of Sydney's hair, but I'm still scared.

His howl turns into laughter. Slowly, we start to laugh, too, disentangling from one another, because it's only Gus pulling a prank on us and because it took him so long to unfold himself from under the low, dirty bunk. He has dust bunnies down the front of his polar fleece, and he still hasn't let go of his bread.

"I couldn't fit all the way underneath that little bed!" He's laughing so hard that he can't get the words out, and I join in. This is how emotions come out of us: in big swoops of expression. It feels good to funnel the fear of the past few days out of my body giggle by giggle.

"Why do you have a hamburger bun?" I ask, gagging on my own fear-spit. "Is that supposed to scare us?"

Gus tears into the bread with sharp teeth, and speaks through a full mouth. "No," he says. "I stole it from the kitchen because I was hungry." He smiles a lupine grin as he ambles out of the cabin, leaving a trail of crumbs, the wood door banging shut behind him.

• • •

That timber wolf never reappears. A week later, Wade thinks that he sees paw prints on the shore of the staff beach. We all run down to see, but after a day of lake weather, nothing is distinguishable except hollows that could have been left by anyone or anything. *Go on*, we say, shoving at Wade's shoulder and laughing, and he laughs, too, no longer completely affected by whatever it was he saw. We link arms with one another and march through the forest to dinner, humming softly. But as we walk, I keep my eyes glued to the trees around us. I look for movement, for a flash of thick white. *Where are you, where are you?* I strain my eyes and look for that something, silent and old, something that sits on its heels and stays still until the sun melts, something that waits and waits and waits to croon that ancient answer: *I'm here, I'm here, I'm here, I'm here—*

THE BUZZ

On the evening we take our staff photos, the lake is calm and the skies are clear. The sun is a blush-pink and orange band on the horizon, and the water has the smallest of chops. It's warm, and welcoming, and the guests are in a good mood. Henry herds us down to the shore after dinner service, so some of us will be photographed in serving whites and wearing makeup, and some of us will be photographed in our green staff shirt with messy hair. We're all ready to make our mark, to document our year and have our own picture hanging on the wall. But there's a bunch of people missing at the moment.

"Wait, where are the guys?" Syd cranes her neck, peering back into the bush, where the paths lead to the guideshack. I can hear a kerfuffle, but can't see anything.

"Oh no," I murmur.

"What the—"

All of a sudden, Jack, Pea, Kev, Aidan, Wade, and Connor, and then even Gus come marching out of the forest. Pantsless.

"Of course!" Alex hollers.

All seven of them sashay down to the shoreline like cabaret dancers, showing off their legs—lighter up at the thigh meat, bronzed and brown down at the calves and ankles—and mincing around as Henry rolls his eyes with an exasperated smile.

"Christ, look at Gus's legs," Syd says, elbowing Emma in the stomach and making her exhale a little with the force of it.

"They're nicer than a woman's," Tiff says, laughing, as the guys line up in a can-can formation and each fling one leg into the air, boxers riding up.

We expected this from Jack, but the other guys aren't usually as forthcoming, and so some of these legs aren't ones we've seen. The ridge of inner thigh, the soft sulcus at the back of the knee, the swell of the calf—all such intimate body parts on display for us and our assessing female gazes. In between our reams of giggles and our fumbled attempts at taking pictures, we eye their bodies, making mental notes, creating rankings in our minds.

Finally, Henry puts an end to the show. "Go put your pants on," he says, half-exasperated and half-capitulating. The guys filter back up the main path to wherever they've left their clothes, but not before Jack, unsurprisingly, pulls down his boxers and moons the rest of the staff. I snap my own picture: he's blurry, wild-eyed and guffawing, looking back over his shoulder, his ass out, the other men clumped around him, grinning the widest I've ever seen them and lit up by the sunset like a bunch of young gods.

·   ·   ·

After weeks together, our interpersonal connections have finally become clearer, honed from hours spent observing one another and listening to gossip and offhand comments. We create a web: Kev seems to have a girl back home who writes him letters, but he maybe likes me, while Emma likes Kev. Jack and Tiff have been dating for years and they share a bunk: they met at the lodge, seasons ago, when Jack was dating someone else. Aubrey has a boyfriend back home. Wade has a maybe-girlfriend, but he seems to have a soft spot for Alex. Alex has a boyfriend, so she spends all her time burrowed in her bunk, writing letters to him. Syd and Connor are sleeping together. Connor has an infant son, and we think that his baby's mother is in her teens, but we can't be sure. Henry has a girlfriend, and when she flies up for a few days, she makes him play Christina Aguilera on the sound system, much to our amusement and delight. I'm single. Emma is single. Robin is single, and so is Aidan. Pea is single, but he dated Alex the year before. Gus has an ex-wife, a new girlfriend, five kids.

This is the way our lodge love lives go: staccato cycles of hormones, a delicate dance around one another in a desperate bid to keep our work lives and personal lives separate. At the beginning of the summer, we were sussing each other out, and so there wasn't room for mania. Now we're too familiar with each other to be aloof. We've seen too much of each other to pretend not to get a flash of heat that pins us in place and makes us rethink the way we look at someone. Sometimes, the wanting is so intense all there is to do is wait it out, teeth clenched and fingernails digging into skin. All of this sexual energy revolves around us like a solar system; we're caught in the thick tautness of it, helpless, suspended.

*   *   *

I feel like I'm burning up. I press my lower belly to the chest freezer in the laundry room to try to relieve the pressure. When we do grocery haul, I ask the dockhands to load my wheelbarrow as much as they can. I read like a crazy woman, chewing through two, three, four books a week, so that I have something to do at night. I clean my bunk. I fold laundry. I sweep the floor. I sort and stack the tangle of shoes that grows in our cabin entranceway. Sometimes, these things help. Most of the time, they don't.

It all comes to a head one afternoon, when Wade and Connor are teasing me as I try to clean the staff dining room table. Wade is at one end of the room, shoving leftovers in his face; Connor is in the doorway, behind me, talking to Wade over my head. They volley comments about the guests, chores for the day, small talk that normally doesn't bother me. But it's hot, and I'm tired, and the dull buzzing in my ears is growing louder. As I turn to sort the staff cutlery, Wade makes an offhand comment about my dishpit outfit. Admittedly, it's a hideous look, with a tattered President's Choice apron tied overtop of worn leggings, orthopedic shoes, thermal socks pulled up my calves. A strange dart of anger shoots through me, up from my stomach and through to the ends of my fingers. Before I know what I'm doing, I've picked up a fork and hurled it at his head from across the room; in the background, I can hear Connor hooting. Wade shields himself with his hands and my aim is shit, so the fork doesn't hit its mark. This is a new emotion: white-hot animal anger, stoked by proximity and desire. Wade and I stare at each other, me with my mouth stupidly open and him with almost an amused look on his face. When I apologize later, we fist-bump. Fishing-lodge problem solving—*all is forgiven, dude.* I'm not worried about him holding a grudge, because it's the first time we've clashed, but I *am* worried about my reaction to simple teasing, and how I couldn't control myself.

This odd aggression becomes hard to contain. It's as though the reins have snapped. I find that when the sun is highest and my arousal peaks with painful acidity, I can no longer control what I once had tabs on. The smallest things set me off—a wayward look, a comment from one of the guys, Henry nagging—and the anger plows through me. That's when I feel like a puppet, and when my body takes over: I fling pieces of kindling at Connor, yell expletives at Kevin from across the shoreline, throw my clean dishes down in the sink so hard that the plastic glasses crack and even Sam backs away.

And then the Beaulieu party arrives.

●　●　●

One night, Emma, Alisa, and I get fed up with the boys' ribbing. "Hey Big Rig, you dumb fuck! You ever going to show us your paper-plate tambourine?" "Which one of you dummies clogged that toilet today?" "Housekeepers are about as useful as a fart in a spacesuit, gee fucking whiz!" We decide to turn in for the evening, starting the despondent trudge from the guideshack back to our cabins.

I'm able to laugh at myself like anyone. But lately, it feels as if the boys' teasing is going too far and crossing over into malice. I understand why. The hot summer days tend to make young men stir crazy and a housekeeper is an easy target. I try my hardest to be a feisty sparring partner—I toss off *fuck yous* faster than anyone, I try to keep up, try not to be a piss-baby and get my feelings hurt—but tonight I'm too tired to fight back. In fact, I feel close to tears.

The three of us walk the dark path in silence, too defeated to even try to prop one another up.

"Hey. Hey! You guys like euchre?"

The Beaulieu party consists of about twenty guys: fathers, sons, uncles, great-uncles, nephews, cousins. They're wealthy and self-made—construction-business managers, grocery-store-chain owners, carpenters—and they're here to party and unwind, not just to catch trophy fish. These are our favourite kinds of guests, people who work to afford the trip and then actually have fun while they're here. Serving a table of people who want to have fun makes my job easier, and I know that the tips will probably be good; serving a table of curmudgeonly, silent fishermen in camo means I'm scrambling to make con-versation, struggling to find common ground, and I usually don't end up with much spending money. The Beaulieus stroll happily into breakfast, they don't rush down to the dock, they're never late for dinner; they always say please and thank you; they laugh a lot—big, whooping chuckles that fill the corners of the dining room and make us smile back in the dishpit.

Most important, there are six young men our age in the Beaulieu party, all of whom are standing outside of Cabin 1, looking at the three of us. Inside the cabin, I can see the glow of the fireplace, their uncles and fathers sitting around the cheap plastic table with playing cards in hand. Everyone is drinking rye or rum, and everyone is shouting good-naturedly. It beckons, so unlike the tenseness we just left behind in the guideshack that my feet almost move of their own accord.

Henry has a strict policy about not mixing with the guests. In our summer contracts, he told us:

> *. . . Light social contact only. Do not get involved with any of the guests. Staff are welcome to chat with guests but conversations should be light and informal. No discussion of politics or religion. Do not question guests about their families or how they make their living. Do not butt into a conversation. The rule "speak only if spoken to" is the spirit of this rule of etiquette. Do not ask to join into an activity with guests (i.e., ask to join a card game or game of darts or pool.) . . .*

Personally, I think that some guests don't want a silent waitress. Instead, they want someone to gasp at the trophy pike they've caught that day, someone to call them out on their bullshit, someone to laugh at their jokes and feed it right back to them. This makes me feel most capable: figuring out how to read people while handing them their oatmeal and bacon, balancing a tray on my hip, remembering their orders without using a notepad. I become a telepath. I divine people's needs and the reasons they decided to escape their city and come to the woods, and then I use what I know to make them happy. When I serve a taciturn Ohioan, I salute him and call him "sir" until he finally cracks a grin and tips me twenty dollars. When I serve a group of miners from small-town Northern Ontario, I let them waltz me across the dining room, keeping my head up as they twirl me around their suntanned legs and up and over their bare feet. Somehow, I already know that the Beaulieu boys are good people, wouldn't try to take advantage of us, wouldn't set us up for a fall.

"Yeah?" Alisa is the one to reply, always the bravest. We stand, far enough away from the boys to be able to run if we need to, and I get a sense of what it must be like for hunters pursuing deer. The guys don't seem to want to move for fear of spooking someone. The dark means we can't see their faces, only their silhouettes lit up by the warmth and jollity behind them.

"We need more players," one of them says, almost shyly. "Do you guys—maybe—do you want to join us?"

I start, half-turned around to get the hell out of there before I do something that Henry could fire me for, but something in his voice stops me. I have a feeling that they've spent the past day and a half trying to figure out how to ask us this question. We're frozen, three velvety does. I can tell that the boys are all sort of smiling.

"Well," Emma exhales.

"Okay." It's my voice that says this, somehow, but it seems to be the magic word because their shoulders relax at the same time as Alisa lets forth her perfect laughter, and the moment is a pact.

The Beaulieu group has booked a number of the cabins in camp, but No. 4 seems to be where all of the young men are staying. When Emma and Alisa and I walk in, the boys run in front of us, strangely polite, pulling out chairs and slamming cups down on the table. This makes us unsure, because we're used to the guys shoving us around and yanking on our braids, trying to stare at our asses and pulling the chairs out from under us to see how hard we fall. By comparison, this is chivalry.

"Do you want a drink?"

I've never had a drink with a guest. Before I can refuse, one of the boys—Hunter—darts from window to window, pulling the drapes shut.

"Look," he says, "I know you're not supposed to be here with us. So we'll lock the door and keep the curtains shut, right? And if Henry knocks on the door for whatever reason, we'll just tell him to . . . to . . . fuck off." The other guys cheer in response to Hunter's words.

I look at Emma and Alisa across the table. We stare at one another from under our eyelashes, trying to communicate without saying a word. *I want this*, I pulse to them. *I really want this.* Emma's mouth twitches; Alisa bobs her head. I look up to the young men who are standing around us, waiting.

"Do you have rye?" Emma asks.

Within two minutes, the three of us are holding rich, strong drinks, and we're being dealt hands of euchre. I assess the young men: Hunter, the rude one, with pierced ears and an abrasive sense of humour. Josh, the quiet one with the out-of-place V-neck T-shirt. Graham, the nice one, smoking pot out of the window. Nate, the one with the face—and body—of an Abercrombie & Fitch model. Jasper, the one all the girls swoon over, quiet and kind and good-looking. Trent, the stocky, handsome one.

Trent catches me looking and waggles his tongue at me. "I'm calling you as my partner, Red."

The night is too short, the time too slippery. We end up staying in their cabin for hours, drinking rye and rum and learning the nuances of euchre. I start to learn their tells and tics. Trent and I become good at bluffing. When Hunter and Alisa bellow *pick it up* and Trent doesn't want the suit to be trump, he clicks his neck from side to side and leans back in his chair with a satisfied smile on his face.

"Aw, yeah. Just what we wanted, eh, Anna?"

"Real good, that suit."

"Fucking *great*!"

● ● ●

We see everything, know everything, gossip about *everything*. Words carry across the lake, so the housekeepers on shore can hear guides coming in and identify them by the swear words they use. If housekeepers are folding sheets in the laundry room, and other girls are making beds in the lodge rooms above, we can chat to each other through the floor. This whole lodge sometimes becomes all about finding spaces to fuck around in, or fuck in, or at least a place in which to tell each other a secret. It can drive a person crazy; I miss having a door to close and lock, a bed that no one can see, a shower that isn't in a shared room. It wears on a person, having every word and action spread out like a feast for others to pick at. The always-togetherness. The eyes constantly watching.

Some of us problem-solve by burrowing away. We use our sleeping bags as shields and try to ignore our damp early-morning dreams when we wake up sticky and disoriented. We nap during our breaks, chase sleep relentlessly, wake up to haul groceries or change the load of laundry over before disappearing again.

Manual labour also diverts: it tricks the brain into forgetting about other evolutionary needs. Because of this, I offer to unclog the scariest of blocked toilets, take pleasure in hearing the sound of pipes sighing in relief. One afternoon, Sydney spends hours cleaning a shower stall with steel wool and Comet powder, sitting on a stool in the bathhouse by herself and scrubbing with frightening determination—she doesn't even let up when I come in to dance a jig and try to distract her. Connor builds a seven-by-seven pyramid of empty oil drums, a structure so tall it rivals the black spruce that serve as its backdrop. Our bodies ache for days after each new project, and we complain to one another, but secretly, we relish the hard work and the distraction.

And sometimes we react by directing our frustration outward, torturing others. During a lake shower one afternoon, I spot Pea and Kevin on shore and flash them. Bodies are part of the fauna here, and all of my roommates have already seen my bits during our morning scrambles. Most of the men have probably seen large swaths of my body, too, because shirts get displaced or sometimes halfway pulled off while lifting loads of lumber, and I'm careless with my skin the way a woman who grows up without young men pursuing her is. I forget sometimes that the men I'm working alongside have sex drives, fantasies, might look at me like a woman and not a girl—and certainly not as a tomboy, one of their own.

Pea notices my naked chest and gives me the thumbs-up. My breasts are so white that he's probably momentarily blinded—if he can even see that far, because I'm a good distance out from the shore. Kev, on the other hand, misses the moment, because he's looking down at the sand for animal tracks.

With no outlet, the crazy energy buzzes up and down our legs and necks, vibrates against the backs of our throats, turns into fingers that don't stop trembling and a body that is always tense. I wonder if we're actually meant to embrace the arousal. To hold it close and try to bridle it, slip a bit in its mouth, make it work for us and not against us. Maybe the constant tautness is necessary; maybe it's the oil that keeps us lubricated and rumbling along in our rote day-to-day chores; maybe it's the one pure thing that circulates through our exhausted systems. I think it might be the force that keeps us from collapsing.

It's one of the reasons I take the front path, along the waterfront, rather than the quiet back path when I'm carting linens to and from the laundry room. Walking the shore means walking by the guys; it means either jeers or catcalls, depending on the day.

"Oh, Big Rig," sung in drawn-out scale.

"Hey, Big Rig," rolled around in a mouth.

"Hey, Anna," Gus yells from where he's sitting in his boat. "Do you know that we had a vote on which of the housekeepers has the best ass? And you won."

"Oh, wow, what an honour," I say, as deadpan as I can manage. "You're old enough to be my father, you know."

There's a burst of laughter as I flip them the middle finger, but I'm smiling behind it and they know I'm not angry. I'll take this over the insults that rip from their mouths on a night when Henry has been short with them and they are in turn short with the girls, rough with the boats, jerky with the motors, loud with the dock box.

"I have laundry to do," I call. There's a load of towels in the washer that desperately needs to be transferred to a dryer, so

I scythe in between the trees and choose the concrete path that leads past the windows of the lodge bar.

The *shick-shick-shick* of rain pants in motion announces his presence before the duck-call voice does.

"Oh fucking Jesus," I say under my breath, turning around to foil whatever Jack has planned. He has a look on his face, the same expression we see when he starts to unbutton his pants, or through our cabin window when he hurls rocks onto our roof.

"I want a piggyback ride," he drawls, clicking his teeth together. He knows exactly how to goad me. He knows that if he asks—tells—me the right way, I won't say no. "I've seen you with a wheelbarrow. You're strong, right?"

"Yeah, okay," I say, half-joking, turning around.

I can feel the moment the air shifts between us as he takes a running start. I don't have time to fend him off. All I can do is brace, and all of a sudden he's on me, so heavy I stumble backward, and the two of us hang in a second of absolute silence, trying not to fall together. My legs are bent and shaking under the weight, our four arms outstretched for ballast, like a multi-limbed boreal god. *Beast with two backs*, my mind suddenly offers, and I fight the urge to shudder.

"*Christ*," I hiss. It's easy to forget, when Jack needles, that he's older than me, broader than me. That, underneath the boyish trappings and irritating jokes, he's a man. He presses his chest to my back; his chin is hooked over my shoulder, his wide, belligerent mouth damp on my ear.

"Bet you can't carry me all the way to the lodge, Big Rig. Why do we call you Big Rig if you're not strong enough to even do that?" He punctuates his point by wrapping his legs around me, slotting his lean calves onto the shelf of my hips.

"Fucking hell, you're heavy," I say. And then I start to walk.

All the wheelbarrowing in the world couldn't have prepared me for the weight of a man on my back, his thighs digging into my waist as he tightens his forearms around my shoulders. I take it one staggering step at a time, focusing on the in and out of my breath, which is syncing up with the strangely comforting one-two of his. We're one snarky entity, two dumb humans pressing against each other. I'm too winded to be rude, and he seems to be too focused on not toppling over to snarl cruelty into my ear.

I pause for a moment, re-hitching his body on my back. He tightens around me like a parasite.

"Jesus Christ, Big Rig, use those birthing hips of yours!"

I dig my fingers into the meat of his calves as a response, and he hisses, and then we both laugh as if we're surprised, and I stumble by the lodge window where, unbeknownst to me, Tiffany has watched the whole exchange.

⁕ ⁕ ⁕

Nine weeks with no sexual activity didn't sound bad when I took the job. It's easy to eschew physical gratification and keep work relationships running smoothly for the sake of the lodge. Who wants to experience a breakup or a meltdown up here? Who wants to come face to face with a pissed-off lover every hour of every day? Better to pull up your bootstraps and keep your clothes securely in place, at least for sixty-seven days.

But that buzz, which at first I thought was some side effect of lack of sleep, starts to shift; it spreads its wide palm over the span of my head, cupping my skull with strange warmth. It becomes a hum in my gut; a quiet ringing in my ears that I only notice when I lie down at night; an elevated heart rate that seems to keep me propelled and manic. I think, at first, that it's fear, that emotion that's linked to my uncertainty, the inability to let my guard down for so many reasons.

But it's not fear. The buzz amplifies with every shower taken in the women's section of the bathhouse, where the outdoor urinals are visible from the windows, where men taking a piss could peek in at us if the curtains aren't drawn properly. It intensifies when I realize that I'm a bit in love with each of the young men on staff, and some of the guests, even some of the fishermen who are far too old for me, white-haired and fatherly. It grows stronger when I realize that even makeup-free and grubby, I'm still, peculiarly, wanted. Sweaty, filthy, or three days without a shower or a hairbrush—it doesn't seem to matter.

This is a strange kind of power I haven't experienced before. Normally, I feel colt-legged and awkward. My dating life has been patchy and mostly painful, and I'm used to being alone. In fact, I mainly enjoy it. But here, something about my uninhibited rudeness, my brusqueness and bare face, makes me someone worth pursuing.

I'm the strongest, rawest version of myself. Without the anxiety that comes from commuting, flirting, trying to be the coquette, putting on blush and lipstick and doing my hair, I have become myself. I'm thoroughly wanted. And I also thoroughly want, spooling in that raw feeling and looping it back around the people who created it. Arousal becomes unharnessed. There's freedom in being uncaring and in being a little bit wild. It's less clichéd than feeling simply sexy. It's not the same as being turned on. Instead, it's related to the raw environment around me. There's a filthiness to having a limited sexuality in a limitless place. It's something primal, related to love.

● ● ●

Emma, Alisa, and I go back to Cabin 4 every night the Beaulieu party stays at the lodge. It becomes an amazing secret. The other staff members know we're up to something, since we're not spending time in the guideshack, and we show up to breakfast tired-eyed and grinning like fools, but they can't quite figure it out.

One night, all nine of us wear hats that we've found in the cabin and in mouldy closets around the lodge: bucket hats, trucker hats, bug-net hats, rain hats. The next night, we play Supertramp as loud as we can, and take turns proving our bravery by touching the electric bug zapper Jasper has brought with him. The following night, we invent a card game called Tequila for Breakfast, a frenetic mashup of the games Signal and Spoons. One night, Emma and I stagger to bed at 2 a.m., and Alisa stays up to watch the sunrise with the six guys, shoulder to shoulder on the rocky shore lip, wide-eyed and beautiful in the burnished early light.

Most of all, we marvel that they never make us feel uncomfortable. Despite the raunchy, twentysomething sexual tension strung tight between our bodies like rope, the guys never make any moves. They don't bug us, even when we're drunk out of our skulls and our defences are lowered. In our cabins, late at night, the girls rank the Beaulieu boys in terms of who we'd have sex with and who we'd pass on. We make the crudest remarks about their bodies and their mouths and their fingers. They probably do the same about us. But when we're all together, we give wobbly, giggling high-fives across the table. We're allies, not competitors. We're friends, not pursuers and prey.

It's as if the Beaulieu boys have been brought to the lodge to make us happy again. We were beginning to get sad and tired. And then these six young men tumbled into our lives, and fed us their fathers' booze, and made us feel human. They don't take us for granted, even though we make their beds every morning and serve them dinners every night. During working hours, we all keep our distance, aside from a few well-placed pinches and sly grins, but when night settles, I run down the back path to their cabin, my red hair flying behind me. I burst through their door and fling myself onto their bunks, ready for another round of euchre. I'm not just a waitress, not just a housekeeper, not just a servant—I'm a friend.

On their last night in camp, the entire Beaulieu group has a wild party. They've printed T-shirts for themselves—beige, baggy things with a picture of a fish (a salmon, incongruously) on the front and a saying on the back: *A woman who has never seen her husband fishing doesn't know what a patient man she married.* Doug, the leader of the pack, gives each of the girls a shirt. When he hands one to me, I feel my eyes fill; I look down at the fabric so that I don't get teased. Later, when it gets dark, every person at the lodge—staff members, manager, guests—goes down to the dock, wearing our new clothes, and we watch Doug set off the feeble fireworks he's brought with him. As each red and green starburst goes off, as the crowd *oohs* and *aahs* appropriately, Emma and Alisa and I move closer to the Beaulieu boys, and the nine of us find one another's hands. In the dark, with all eyes looking up to the sky and our fingers interlaced, I feel strong again.

When their group leaves on a hungover grey morning, we fly into their arms before they get on the plane, even though Henry's watching us. Those six Beaulieu boys pick us up, one at a time, me and Emma and Alisa, and they spin us around, murmuring platitudes in our ears, telling us how good we are, how strong we are, how they'll never forget us or this summer or this lake or those card games. We try not to cry into their necks. We bow our heads so Henry doesn't see the way our eyes glitter. We promise to stay in touch, but somehow, I know that I'll never see those beautiful boys again.

* * *

The next day, I sit at the picnic table and look down at the guys pulling boats for the umpteenth time this summer. They're the same as always—rude and rough, loud and joking, shoving each other and yelling half-insults in my direction. I'm trying to read, but all I've done for the past ten minutes is trace and retrace the same paragraph with my eyes. My six new friends have left, and I feel dull and forgotten. The mottled, colourless sky doesn't help my mood. The final two weeks of the summer seem to stretch out in front of me, matte and humourless, and

I wonder how, without nightly euchre games, without strong rye and swing dancing between the bunks of Cabin 4, I'll slog through.

There's a shout a few feet away from me, and my attention moves from the book in my lap to the way the boys have straightened up and are looking out at the horizon, their hands raised. I squint to see what they're motioning to when the air pricks with static; the hair on my arms tilts to the side and then stands straight up. I've never felt something as immediate. Something slippery and animal inside of my body curls up, my guts aware of the impending change in weather before my brain is. My gaze snaps from the horizon back to the boys, and in that one eerie moment, they all slant their heads at the same time, as though hearing something I can't.

I've never seen the boats pulled in storm weather. I've heard talk about it, how guests sometimes get roped into helping if they're around and if the dock is short-staffed because guides are still coming in off the lake. But caught out of the cabin, this is the first time I'll see it for myself. The rising wind ruffling the hair around Wade's nape. The slight colour of panic in Aidan's eyes.

The boys file into a line, hustling toward the first boat. And then they stop, right below my legs.

Jack peers up, looking at me. The rest of the boys stand behind him, legs akimbo. I shift, widen my thighs—*let him ask for it*, that raw part of my brain entreats. The boys' eyes are volatile in the dim light. Rain is coming fast. Even I can tell; I can smell the storm on the shoulder bones of the thick wind that is curling my hair around my head. The meat of my mouth swells with the rising electricity in the air. The other girls are

spending their night off in their cabins, wrapped around magazines and headphones, but I remain outside, stubborn. Tomboy,
rebel, fool. Explorer.

Jack rolls his tongue around. I see it through the skin of his
cheeks.

Ask for it, ask for it, beg.

"Wanna help?"

The shore is bare; I'm the only one around. Where are the
guests? Caught out? Back in their rooms? I didn't notice them
come in, didn't notice them walk by. What have I been doing?

Yes. I want to. I want to help.

"There's only one rule for boat pull," Jack continues. "Don't
fall."

"If you fall," Aidan repeats for Jack, speaking to me like I'm
an idiot, "we hump you." He speaks gleefully, his face speckled
with wet clay from the waterline, and the storm starts to unfurl
itself behind his head, moving across the lake. I can see the
lightning from where I'm standing on the far shore. I forgot
about that crude boat-pull ritual—if someone is clumsy enough
to trip and fall while pulling, the other boys shriek and pile on
top of the victim, thrusting their hips. *Humping.* I roll my tongue
in my mouth, too, tasting the request. Jack stares. Aidan laughs,
a harsh sound like the wind, and Gus joins in.

All of a sudden there are too many things to concentrate
on. Don't slip on the wet rails. Don't get your leg trapped under
the boat. Don't stop pulling no matter what because if you stop
someone else will have to take on all your weight, and injuries
could happen. And now don't fall, even on the dry, safe shore,
because if you do—if *I* do—I get swarmed. I fail.

But this is electric. My spine feels straight again. The sky is steel and swirl and silver, the clouds ripe stones about to tumble into one another and split apart over our heads. How could I have ever thought this was only one colour, something flat and unappealing? My palms sweat; my eyes are wide. And then I slither out of my seat, scud down onto the shore in one hurried movement, all limbs, and land in front of them, my hands on my hips. Jack nods.

"Grab the rope," Pea says over his shoulder as he walks to the first boat.

I stand shoulder to shoulder with the boys, staring at the canoes in front of us. I think to myself that from out on the water, from the vantage point of the storm, we all look the same: dressed in the same colour, heads bent the same way, necks tight with anticipation and desperate laughter. I can smell our end-of-day bodies—shadfly moult, briny hair, dust and grime— and as we shift and tighten the ropes in our hands, we feel one another's muscles slacken and respond like lake waves. I'm at the waterline, my feet on the sacred boys' ground; my hands are around the boat rope, palms carving a new path. Pete straightens up near the back of the boat, and as he opens his mouth, I twist the rope around my hands. I huddle into Jack and Gus and hope that one day I'll get to touch the gunwales, maybe get to skitter across the rails, too. I hope that I become nimble, that I don't fall, that Henry doesn't come and see me hunkered down with the boys and tell me to piss off back to the upper shore. I hope that I can pull as well as they do, and then Pete starts to count and we breathe together, an intricate braid of bodies, and then we pull.

NO TO IT ALL

"Hey, fuckers," Jack calls. "You want a job to do?"

Syd and I are sitting at the staff picnic table; I'm trying to read and she's writing letters home. Both of us are tired as hell, and Jack's voice is as jarring as a jay's. I roll my eyes and Syd snorts beside me, refusing to look at him and Pea where they're hovering over us. Jack knows that Sydney and I aren't technically supposed to be doing work, not until tomorrow morning, but he also knows that of all the housekeepers, we're the rudest and the most competitive. We'll stand up to the guys, even if it draws us into a stupid argument. We don't take shit from anyone. In fact, the other morning, Syd accidentally stumbled upon and then demanded to join the daily—and until then, secret—5:30 a.m. men's staff breakfast. Up until that moment, this meal was a ritual for the older male workers. Murphy intimated she should leave. *No girls allowed*—the unspoken rule. Sydney turned to him, without hesitation, and said, "Murphy, I don't give a fuck," drawing out the last word so that the vowel stretched over two rich syllables. She told me that everyone was silent, gaped at her, and then Gus shoved over so she had a space at the table. Now Murphy secretly loves her, and she'll get early-morning breakfast whenever she wants for the remaining days up here—better-quality bacon, sunny-side-up eggs, and Texas toast.

Syd flips Jack and Pea the bird, already on the defensive. "What do you want, peckerheads?" I smile behind my book.

"See that picnic table your fat asses are sitting on?"

I look down. "Yeah. So what?" I can sense what's coming, but I'm going to make these peckerheads work for it. Let them say it out loud so we can draw this game out. I've lowered the book; my stupid grin is visible, and I can see Pea trying not to smile over Jack's shoulder.

"It has to be moved to the staff beach. You lazy housekeepers have nothing to do. Why don't you do it for me?" Jack is also full-out grinning by now.

We absolutely, positively don't have to do this chore. It's our downtime, and this edict isn't coming from Henry, so it's not an actual task. And considering the staff beach is on the other side of the point, we'll have to drag the table down a few hundred feet of path, and it isn't a light load. But Jack has prodded at our pride and I don't want to be seen as lazy. Somehow, I want his approval. And we're so loopy and giggly-throated, there might be something funny about this.

Syd and I parrot at the same time: "Oh, damn you." "It's our night off!"

Jack cocks his head. If Henry had asked us, we would have refused, but we know that we're going to do it. Now it's just the coquettish dance, the pretending to refuse, the needling to ask us again, the power exchange. It's an iteration of flirtation, this give-and-take action, the in and out.

"We don't have to," we say, sing-song, flipping the ends of our hair. The coquetry is all the more off-putting because we're greasy-faced, wearing paint-splattered pants and smudged sunglasses. We stink of sweat and young woman, the best kind of perfume.

"Prove you're strong."

"Say please."

"Fuck no!"

So we move it. Or at least we try to. The table is so cumbersome we can only pick it up and carry it a few feet at a time. Neither Syd nor I want to be walking backward, so we continually switch places. As we drag it, Jack walks alongside us, half-bent over, jeering at us, egging us on like some twisted bench boss, and we all start laughing so hard that we end up dropping the table over and over again. At one point, I have to sit and put my head in my hands. It's the kind of laughter that comes from the deepest part of the body, and it's the kind that can't be stopped. It explodes up through the mouth and the nose, and trying to catch a breath only stokes it. By the time we get to the edge of the staff beach, Syd and I are bent over, actual tears streaming down our faces. I'm close to pissing my pants, I'm so uncontrollable. We have to leave our load there, and Jack and Pea end up carting the table down the last few steep feet to the sand. They lift it with ease, moving far faster than Sydney and me, and they roll their eyes as they pass us, but the two of us can barely find a moment to care, because we're literally on the ground, helpless with mirth, like we're under some sort of spell. We grab at each other's arms and shoulders, wiping at our faces with the heels of our hands until Jack and Pea come and stand over us.

"Fucking animals," Jack says, shaking his head, but I think I can hear a wisp of something other than disgust behind his words—something like respect, or at least tolerance.

• • •

Away from Kesagami, Jack and I wouldn't look twice at each other; we wouldn't even be friends. He relishes small-town slang, makes homophobic, racist, and misogynist jokes too often for me to count. He hates Toronto; hates any big city for no obvious reason, maybe because he's scared of them. He has an eerie ability to assess a person and see their fraying seams— and then take advantage by lashing his words into those weak spots until his prey splinters. Most of the girls on staff just roll their eyes at Jack and push past him. I'm the one who lets him in, and he uses this entranceway to wipe his feet and make himself at home.

The only time Jack is consistently tolerable is when he's interacting with Tiffany. I like watching him and Tiff speak, because they're startlingly tender with each other, and I like when someone's better half throws their usual demeanour into harsh contrast. Tiff humanizes Jack, and if she wasn't here, he would be unbearable—or maybe he would be in my bed.

But I don't want to date Jack. I want to engage him; I want him to challenge me. It's so rare that I meet someone who will fling my rhetoric back at me without blinking; here is someone who is my verbal match, who won't hesitate to take me down a peg or three. It's disgustingly thrilling to be excoriated by him, to have someone to spar with. I just want to spend as much time as I can trading barbs with him, watching the way his mind works, learning the ways he picks people apart and examines them, because I know that once we go back to our respective cities, our friendship will end in that slow, awkward way that happens when two people have nothing tangible in common.

Jack's hooks aren't barbless. He knows how to inflame, and he knows how to toss out something so devastating that his words stay lodged in your mind for hours, days, weeks after the fact. There are many times throughout the summer he's done that with all of us—he teases Sydney after she's had a particularly bad breakout by asking her if she shaves her face with a broken bottle in the mornings, and she's so hurt that she doesn't talk to him for days; he insists on continuing to call Robin "Flush," ever since she clogged that toilet, and she hates it but won't tell him otherwise—but one afternoon, he crosses a line.

Syd and I are at the staff table, trying to relax. The sun spreads across our skin; our shins and palms, which used to be creamy and well-tended before this summer, are criss-crossed with scabs and calluses. I pick at my nails. When I put my hand to my face, I smell bleach, cooking oil, and dirt. When I close my eyes and let the wind up under the weight of my hair, let the sun warm my cheeks, I feel human again, despite the grub and grime. True, we're all reluctant for the summer to end, but at the same time, we can't wait to get back to our respective homes, private showers, hair salons, fresh milk in our coffees, plush mattresses. Every day of the countdown feels like a tightrope walk. Feeling two emotions at once, every single minute of every waking hour, has me strung tightly, wound up and more fragile as the days march on.

"Hey," Jack snaps from the shoreline. Syd and I both open our eyes slowly.

"What do you want?" Syd's voice sounds soft. It's one of those days where we've already been pushed around by bossy guests and bossy Henry and bossy Sam, where we're so bone-aching tired that we're not even watching the boys, not jeering at them. Sitting on the shoreline is always a gamble on days like these, because the boys could be balm or bombast. We were hoping for balm, but it seems like it's going to be bombast.

Jack saunters closer to where we're sitting. He's full of swagger; I wonder if it's been a bad day for him, too, because something about the set of his shoulders and the slant of his lips gives him away. The boys trail him like mindless beasts, glee-eyed and almost drooling with some degenerate group-think. *Pack mentality*, I think. I hold myself still, like a piece of prey might. I hate myself for it.

"Every time we pull boats," Jack says, soft enough to be threatening but loud enough so all his acolytes can hear, "it's you ugly fuckers sitting there and watching us."

So far, I've mostly kept my cool this summer, as has Syd. As have most of us. Anger usually lasts for a few bright seconds and then fades quickly. It's the nature of things at the lodge—angry staff members don't work well together. We're normally too tired or too busy to be mad. This time, however, my gut contracts. As I stare down at Jack's grinning face, I see the way he's high-fiving the other boys thinking he's really clever, really strong and brave and hilarious for taking the two of us down on a day we were already feeling small, and a mixture of rage and grief, a prickly, cold kind of heat, spreads from the soles of my feet and my groin and under my arms. Rage at his stupidity and sheer meanness; grief at the fact that we seemingly still haven't garnered his respect, despite working hard, despite laughing at his jokes, despite trying over and over again. Syd and I hadn't been doing anything except sitting and talking with each other. This is unprovoked, and it feels like a true attack.

Jack stands, legs spread, on the shore, his too-wide mouth floating in a sharp smile against the background of the water, and his expression is such a potent mix of pride and ignorance that I want to barf. It's bad enough when he understands the impact his words have on us; it's ten times worse when he doesn't. The other boys huddle in a loose circle, giggling behind their hands like children, all of them watching us to see our reactions.

Sydney and I look at each other again. In a testament to our closeness and how well we know each other, we stand up at the same time, trying to hide our hands, which are shaking with anger. Without speaking, we pivot jerkily, turning on our heels and picking up our books and pens and papers with fast fingers. I'm rattling around so badly that I move quickly, so as not to let on how upset I am. Showing weakness paints a target on your chest. It's like dealing with our resident bears: don't let them see you scared; don't show them your back for too long. Jack's voice follows us along the path: *Oh, now you're offended. Oh, now you're pissed, eh?* His jeering fades as we start to run.

As I round a corner, I bump into Gus, who catches me reflex-
ively. I flail in his arms as he tries to hold me out at arm's length.

"What the hell is wrong?"

All I want to do is collapse into his arms and weep, use him
as a pseudo-father figure and be comforted. Instead, I brush
past him, my mouth opening and closing after I stammer *Jack,
boys, Jack*, ignoring his genuine concern.

Later that night, I lie in my bunk, the net pulled tight around
my mattress. The other girls are puttering around, passing a
bag of candies back and forth. I read and reread the same page
in my book, my hands finally steady after hours of breathing
deeply and keeping my face in my pillow. I'm confused about
what happened today and how to handle it for the rest of the
time we have left. My pride wants to keep me from ceding to
Jack, but the logical side of my brain tells me that perhaps what
he said wasn't the most offensive thing, and maybe the heat and
exhaustion is just getting to me. I know he won't be the one to
apologize—I've never seen him say sorry to anyone on staff,
ever. Emotions are so blurred that I can't tell if I'm being rea-
sonable or not, and it disturbs me.

Suddenly, I look up. Outside of the front window, two green
ball caps are bobbing, visible through the dirty screen. Two
dockhands or guides, frozen in place in front of our door. My
gut squeezes.

"Sydney—open the door."

She looks at me with a piece of candy in her mouth, confused by the urgency in my voice. But I know what needs to be
done. If they walk by without knocking, this situation is going
to fester. If we force the scene, we may be able to lance the boil.

She hesitates.

"*Right now.*" My voice has such an edge that all the girls in the cabin snap their heads around, trying to squint to see me through the film of the net.

Sydney flings open the door so hard that it bounces off of the outside wall and the sound is like a gunshot.

There, standing right outside of our cabin, are Jack and Pea. Their hands are in their pockets. Pea has a patient look on his face. Jack looks as close as I've ever seen to sheepish, which is still very far from it.

"Hi," Robin says, looking up at them as she flicks through a magazine. Alisa, who is visiting from her cabin, moves from where she's perched on the bench so that they have space to sit. Sydney blinks, stone-faced. My net covers my face like a veil. I don't lift it as I raise my palm in a lukewarm greeting.

They filter in and sit down. Pea sits quietly as Jack starts talking, loud-voiced, about his day. Filler conversation. I stay quiet, too—the ten count, a fighter biding her time. I let him keep swinging frantically. Finally, during a moment when he takes a breath, there's silence. It sticks to all of us. Jack looks at me, but I know he can't quite make out my expression because of the white netting. Regardless, I raise my eyebrows at him.

"So?" I ask.

"*Fuck.* Sorry," he says. There's a whooshing feeling inside of me, like all of my stress has disappeared. That's all I wanted; it's the perfect apology. Then the conversation moves onward as Pea artfully steers us in a different direction and starts talking about perch, and we start passing around bags of sweets and cans of pop. That's the way of the lodge.

Pea leaves us around eleven o'clock to get ready for bed, but Jack doesn't, and time flies as we talk. Emma, Syd, Robin, and I are lying in our bunks, and Alisa is sitting beside Jack, eating dried apricots and trying to chew between shrieks. Jack is explaining irrigation systems. We've already covered such topics as the Iroquois Confederation, the slow death of the honeybee, pig shit, Mister Twister jigs, and René Descartes. It's late, but the conversation is too good, and we zigzag from one subject to another with only guffaws to bookmark our history.

"Bullshit! Bullshit!" I call Jack on some grandiose statement, and he hurls a piece of candy at me. Alisa laughs beside him, her contagious hiccupping giggle, and then, suddenly, the door swings open.

Tiffany doesn't say anything, only stands in the doorway, framed by the deep velvet dark of the forest behind her, and squints into the brightness of the cabin, looking at our faces, focusing on mine last, and then swinging her head to stare at Jack for one hot, trembling moment. As quickly as she arrived, she turns and leaves, slamming the door behind her with full force.

"Hey, Tiff." Alisa's sunny greeting trails off, and it's punctuated by the sharp slam of the door. "Wait, what?"

The mood changes so quickly it's like the Kesagami weather. Jack stands up, suddenly sober. The rest of the girls don't know what just happened, but I do. We stay quiet as he turns off the light and leaves. We all roll over in our bunks and try to talk ourselves to sleep, but something feels wrong.

For the entire next day, Tiffany won't talk to me, and I know that I've become the enemy.

. . .

A day later, I stand on the steps of the guideshack, trying to get into the building to drop off Aidan's laundry, when the door opens and Jack's standing on the step above me, blocking my way. I didn't realize he had an on-shore day today. I'm torn between shoving past without acknowledging him, or turning and running away.

"Fuck." There's nothing else to say.

He shifts his weight, quiet for once.

"Get out of my way." I climb up a step and try to bump him to one side with my hips. My arms are full with the laundry basket, and he knows that he has me at a disadvantage.

"No."

"You are so goddamn annoying."

"Yep."

"Why aren't you out on the water today?"

"On shore."

This abbreviated conversation is doing nothing for my evaporating patience. I flare, an ember fanned by him. I set my jaw, and we stare at each other. *Move*, I think, and my emotions are so loud, so splayed across my face, that he laughs and I can see the points of his incisors.

No, his body says, definitely. No to so many things.

I almost buckle, but can't. "Get out of my way." I know that I'm bordering on childish now, one pout away from a foot stomp. This is why I'm going to lose—both our argument and, eventually, this friendship. I don't become or stay a woman around Jack: I revert to teenaged sass and, if he's especially cutting, childhood tactics. Somehow, Jack wears his immaturity well. People laugh at his jokes. My immaturity turns me into a nag, a bitch.

I try to push through him, using the basket as a battering ram. All I need to do is get to the door and I'll be home free. But he grabs my upper arms with both hands. I stop moving as he touches me, as his fingers wrap around my biceps.

Before I can thrash away from his dirty palms, he pushes me down the steps with just enough force that I'm propelled backward in a stumble, and not enough force that I fall. All I can see is his mouth bobbing, rich and open. All I feel is distress. I can't get to the door; there's no handle for me to grasp. Jack grins a pike's grin. If he wanted to, I'd let him push me all the way down, down to the pine needles, down to the hot granite. But instead he stands at the top of the stairs, legs planted and spread, arms crossed over his chest.

ROOTS

There are two sides to this place. There's the lodge and everything that comprises: the hub of ramshackle buildings, the straggly paths that connect everything, the generator and oil drums and buoys and the wood splitter. Here, there's the noise of human sprawl and takeover, a flesh-and-blood cacophony: the servers' panicked squawking over the thrumming of the kitchen fans, the sound of one housekeeper hollering to another from Cabin 6 to the motel, the dockhands yelling down on the shoreline during boat pull, Sam hovering at the top of it all, screaming at our ineptitude.

The other side of Kesagami comprises the pieces of land where we haven't spread ourselves. There's a point where the paths end and the woods begin, where I can take fifteen or twenty steps forward and the sound changes, where the trees are so dense that the quilt of background noise—boat motors, the low-hanging rumble of supply planes coming in, and the yelping, squealing, giggling, yelling, crying—becomes no-noise. Something that expands and contracts on its own.

Something that exists: patient, malicious, brooding, angry, wise, old.

We can't conquer what surrounds us. We chop firewood and nick the forest apart for kindling, but we know that when it comes down to it, the trees have been here longer than we have, and we will never, ever get the best of them. The woods are beautiful, but it's also the place that makes me feel the most uncomfortable: I feel safe and unsafe; I feel at home and at the same time so frightened I can barely wait to turn tail and run out of there. That's the dichotomy of this place. It's either spend time with everyone, always, snared in the cyclone of noise and sensation and everyone's eyes on you and every emotion that dances across your face, or it's the forest. The wild or the wilder. The present or the past. It's a screaming mess of noise, or dangerous quiet.

For young people like us, who think we're so goddamn important, silence can be scary. We try to fill it; we stay up late to do so. This is why sleep is so difficult to sink our fingers into. The fear of missing out has gotten stronger now that there's just a handful of days left, because we've started to realize that we're going to be leaving and that this place, so removed and so precious, is going to be torn away from us as soon as we get on the plane back to Cochrane. So sleep starts to come second to time spent in one another's presence, bunks, arms. This means, though, that when we flick back through pictures of ourselves on one another's cameras or catch an unexpected glimpse of ourselves in the lake or a mirror we're cleaning, we groan. A lot of us don't recognize ourselves, for many reasons. Our bodies are different. We look honed and defined; the puppy fat from the beginning of the summer has melted away from weeks of hard work. We've gone from pale and pasty to farmer tanned, skin darkened from days out in the sun and on the water. Our muscles are leaner and longer and more corded from weeks of pushing wheelbarrows and lifting rocks and pulling boats.

My body has become tighter and stronger, my shoulders defined and hollowed, and my forearms bronzed. At the same time, I feel like I'm falling apart, an adage that I never quite understood until I came here. I creak. My bones snap when I wake up in the morning. My hips pop in and out of place with a sick and fascinating thunk. My fingernails are shredded; my throat is constantly sore; my back is knotted so badly that I can barely lie flat on the floor before my sacral muscles spasm. I didn't know my meat was so tender, that an environment could run so roughshod over me. But at the same time, the masochist in me delights in it—the dull, sweet ache after a day of physical work is a pleasure I've never known before.

And I'm so tired. We're all so tired. In a way, it makes us beautiful. Our eyelids are purple, our grins manic, and somewhere behind the fatigue, if an observer were to look really hard, they'd see us existing completely and exquisitely. But mostly, we're teetering on the edge of being ready to keel over and fall asleep.

In the middle of all this, a fierce love has developed. I didn't really expect this. It seemed counterintuitive that tenderness should exist in between the ups and downs, but it does. In between the wheelbarrows and the floor-mopping and the nights spent in one another's bunks, there's no space for pretense; the fat is trimmed, and we have become only emotion and instinct. We've all become a little baser, a little more feral in our sleeplessness, and it shows in the way we move among one another.

The girls like to lie in their beds and talk about the boys. The boys like to lie in their beds and talk about the girls. Body parts are compared and ranked like we're drafting teams. We may have started out naive and nervous, but now we stare. We look without guilt or tact. We desire. But it's more than just attraction. We adore one another unequivocally, in the way people thrown together in a harsh environment develop love, but we'd never cop to feeling soft. This love gives us power to make it through the days without collapsing, but somehow, saying it out loud is weakness. We like napping in one another's bunks, but we leave zero trace behind when we wake up for our afternoon shifts. We'll help one another with chores, but we won't say thank you. We love one another, but we're not going to fucking admit it.

It's a disturbing love, something that's simultaneously fraternal and sexual. Sometimes I glance at the dockhands and think of what it would be like to have hushed sex in a staff cabin. Sometimes, I think about pinning one of the boys to the laundry-room door and kissing until a housekeeper has to interrupt us to get a hock of beef out of the chest freezer beside the dryer. Sometimes, I think about being tackled in the shallows of the lake as I take a makeshift bath to try to get clean between the never-ending chores. Girls and boys, brothers and sisters, adversaries and lovers—we're all of these things, noisy and annoying and carving our own path out on this hard land while existing completely soft-hearted with one another.

* * *

Because the bathhouse has walls that don't reach up to the ceiling, the boys and girls are able to speak to each other over the sound of the spray when we shower at the same time. We think it's coy and funny to have conversations with each other while naked, sliding soapy hands over our bodies. Only a little self-restraint and a thin wooden wall separate us from one another.

When the guests go out to fish and we're left alone on shore, we sprint in twos to get clean, our towels flapping behind us like streamers. Sometimes the boys shuck shirts on the way, bursting into the bathhouse half-clothed, panting for soap, mouths open for water. We tell each other jokes as we test the temperature of the spray with our wrists. We complain about our bunkmates as we run hands up and down our legs, slide our fingers between our toes. It's a confessional. We take advantage of it, releasing emotional burden along with the grease of hard physical work.

At first, there was something blithe and innocent about this ritual. We were naked together, but not together. By the end of the summer, however, I try to finagle it so that I'm showering alongside the guys I find most attractive. The ones whose pale calves and shoulders I want to see most in that moment between swinging open the shower door and readjusting the towel. I race to try to emerge clean at the same time. I want to make eye contact. For some reason, this makes me feel like the potential is endless. We only ever stare at each other for a moment, taking in newly shaved ankles, clean toenails, uncombed hair that sits floppy and damp over tanned foreheads. Then we turn and skitter away.

And there lies the problem. We want to, but we won't. We continue to hold back for many reasons—self-preservation, a mutual aim to keep the lodge operating without romantic wrinkle, the way we smell after working for two days straight. But most of all, want has to take a back seat to need, and whether we realize it or not, we need family here more than anything else.

We're so aware of the temporary nature of our work that we feel panicky and weightless in our bodies. We didn't want to make connections, but now we know that we've put down roots here. We didn't want to see what's underneath the clothes because we won't be able to say goodbye, but we did, we saw it, almost all of it. And we know that when we leave here, we'll never again be able to recreate this. Our lake, our lodge, will be different when different people come back to it. Things will have grown over, changed and branched out. This place won't be ours. And we'll never face this dichotomy again: back in real life, brothers are brothers, sex is sex, and the two don't ever cross, and no amount of calling to one another—*Are you there? It's me*—changes that. If we feel disturbed by what we've considered and created, we never say it. This is the only place in the world where I earn an older brother who I want to kiss. *I'm here.*

* * *

Pea entreats us. "Come on," he says, motioning to the vague beyond, the land behind. Some of the housekeepers are sitting on the picnic table by the dock, trying to absorb vitamin D, trying to conserve energy by moving as little as possible.

Alex turns her head and eyes Pea with that specific and beautiful mix of languor and disdain that girls have patented and that the dockhands hate so much.

"Where to?" She leans her head back and her throat is exposed to the sun. In this moment, I can see why the boys become so exasperated with us. We're the condescending demi-gods, aware and unaware of our sensuality. Our hormones push at the boundaries of our bodies, and we don't rein them in. We float our feelings on the wind to the boys, but at the same time we're rude and haughty in the way that only twentysomethings can be. And we're lazy when we want to be—outwardly, pushily lazy. Lazy on the beach. Lazy in public. We don't want to do the work, and we're going to make damn sure that Pea knows it.

Pea sighs, long-suffering and calm. He jerks his head. Back, way back. *Shit.*

"Shit."

"Wood haul."

"*Shit!*"

The trees of Northern Ontario don't get enough credit. These are not the glimmering, graceful birch of Georgian Bay, or the legendary sequoias of the West Coast. These trees don't look pretty. Their forest is not lined up in the telltale even slats of a hand-planted Southern Ontario thatch. These trees haven't had it easy. There's no deep, rich soil to dig their roots into, no lush seasons of rain and temperate weather to ensure their growth. Soil in the boreal forest is incredibly acidic, because conifer needles have high levels of acid, and in rainstorms, this drips from them into the dirt and leaches nutrients deeper into the ground and out of plants' reach. So these trees have fought for every bit of their height and breadth. Their lives aren't defined by leaps and bounds, but a game of inches.

The Jack pine, also known as the grey pine or the scrub pine, is a funny-looking tree. It's often crooked, or even shrub-sized, because of poor growing conditions, and it's largely considered a weed species. It's scrappy and small and was mostly ignored by lumber companies until its larger cousins were overharvested. But it's incredibly tenacious, and it's built to withstand—and even flourish in—the most dangerous of taiga threats: the fire. Jack pine seedlings germinate most successfully in the kind of soil that occurs after a fire rips through the boreal forest; they flourish when the other trees around them have been razed and the sun is visible; they can survive drought conditions for a month or even longer. And, most remarkable of all, their pine cones are designed to bloom open in the fiercest of heat, rather than explode: in fact, it's been noted that Jack pine cones can withstand heat of up to nine hundred degrees Celsius, and the seeds stay undamaged.

So it doesn't feel right to carve up any of these trees, not after they've fought so damn hard. It doesn't feel good to build our woodpiles, to flaunt them by moving them, to trespass with the express goal of taking and taking without giving. But it has to be done, even though we don't like it. We might not feel that it's right, but the four of us—Tiff, Alex, Aubrey, and myself—pull on tight long-sleeve shirts and gloves. We bring out bug-net caps and tuck our pants into our socks. Far back in the forest, away from the hum of the main building, the bugs are even worse; despite the heavy, wet heat, it's better to be covered up.

Here is where the two sides of Kesagami meet, when we—squawking and complaining and loud, from our bitching voices to the sound of fabric on fabric as we swat uselessly at the mosquitoes—enter the deep forest. At first, we don't notice the change around us. Pea leads us back to the hollow, and most of us concentrate on avoiding the sucking wet beneath our feet. But as the walking gets harder, our complaining diminishes, and we grow quieter and quieter. I start to focus on my breath: the humidity fills my nostrils, pushes its way down the back of my throat and into my gut. The heat is so acute—amplified by the heavy clothes we're wearing and the way our cuffs are tucked into socks and gloves—that sweat pools between my breasts and starts to run down the insides of my thighs. I can see the way my co-workers' shoulders are sagging already, and we're not even at our destination.

Everything around me is so goddamn vivid. The moss is a bright, light lime green I've never seen before, plush and foreign to the touch; the spruce needles, when broken underfoot, let off a scent that I've never smelled, dry and sweet and pungent; everything, the detritus, the leaves, the brush, the path, is all new and silent and yet not silent, all of it painted from a palette of rich, rare browns and greens, colours that I think I've seen but now realize I never have.

As I take another step, my foot sinks into the earth with a luscious squelching sound. The ground is spongy, and my running shoe is soaked through. As I pull my foot free, I howl, and the other girls join in, high-stepping as best they can, but knowing that they're fighting a losing battle: we're in a territory that isn't even remotely ours—spruce territory, fen underfoot, the land of muskeg.

The term *muskeg* comes from the Cree word *maskek*. It can be defined as a "grassy bog"—an accurate umbrella term for the eclectic series of landforms that make up this stuff that's halfway between earth and water. It's unstable land, with living plants on top, and plant waste below. Muskeg seems to defy precise definition. It looks crazy and mixed up, composed of mazes of tamarack and spruce, clumps of peat, sedges; the terrain is alien, hilly and rolling and filled with depressions and ditches and pools of motionless water. Muskeg is made up mostly of sphagnum moss, a plant genus that's ninety million years old. Sphagnum grows slowly over decades. Once it reaches critical mass, it controls water flow in and out of its habitat: it can even restrict water to other plants, choking out the competition. Not only that, but the moss acidifies its environment. It cuts off oxygen. The air starts to smell like putrefaction, thanks to the "swamp gas." The environment becomes solely sphagnum—master of its domain.

Canada has more than one million square kilometres of muskeg, with the densest tract of it—as broad as five hundred kilometres in some places—spanning from around the tip of James Bay up across the country, northwest, ending at Great Bear Lake, in the Northwest Territories. Where we are, the muskeg is patchy, not quite all encompassing, which means we can kind of walk through it, but not gracefully. By the time we get to our destination, we're practically oozing our way through the bog, grumpy, hot, damp-footed. And a little bit quieter, a little bit more reverent, in the face of the forest we don't see all that often.

Kev has already been here with his chainsaw, and I see the fruits of his labours: neatly sliced hunks of raw black spruce, perfectly cut rounds. We form a chain, one girl to every five feet, and eye one another with determination. Now is not the time to moan or joke. This is a delicate procedure in which a flinch can result in a log to the face, and as comical and slapstick as that sounds, no one wants to be picking splinters out of their lips. It takes both arms to cradle one chunk of spruce, and our knees bend a little with the weight, our feet sinking into the muck. Pea stands nearest to the pile of wood, and throws the first piece to Aubrey, who throws it to Alex, who throws it to me. I throw it to Tiff, and she loads it into the wheelbarrow.

We're silent, concentrating on keeping the rhythm—the soft sucking of our feet in the ground when we catch the wood, the rough sound of bark on fabric as we pivot at the waist and throw it on. I imagine it's hypnotic to see us pivot and return, silent as sentinels, but in reality it's one of the hardest chores I've ever done, in one of the most compelling and unsettling places I've ever seen. We're part of this now, our limbs stretching out for each log, our feet planted on the ground. We turn and catch, turn and catch, our arms reaching for one another, and I realize that even when we leave, part of us will stay here. Part of us will have taken root.

THE SPARK

A week before leaving, and I'm finally not scared to swim alone. I've learned how to be by myself, with the background sounds and smells of the forest and the shoreline and my own imagination to fill in the gaps. After so many days of cheek-to-jowl living, it's a rare pleasure to be able to dart away for a little bit to wash the heat off my skin. It feels good to be fine with aloneness. There's even something reassuring about the trees: they stand as quiet witnesses as I strip down to my bathing suit and spend a moment with my eyes closed and my face to the sun. How long will it be before I feel this breeze on my skin again, before I feel this sand below my feet? The thought of leaving and maybe never returning to see this beach, this lake, this place is suddenly too much for me, and I walk into the water as quickly as I can manage with the rocks underfoot. As soon as it's deep enough, I bob under, graceless and desperate for some relief, to hide my face and wet the corners of my eyes before the tears can.

Because of the high midday sun, the water is the colour of old blood, rusty, prismatic in rich browns and deep reds, glittering with minerals from the sand I've dredged up. It means I can't see if there's anything lurking alongside me. But I don't care today. I've learned to abandon some of that baseless fear. Yes, be scared—know that there are pike in the lake, bears in the woods, things that could harm you, might eventually want to hurt you—but don't be afraid. Don't let your biases and irrationalities take over and ruin what could be the best summer of your life.

As much as I've dreamed about going back to the "real world," I'm not quite ready. I'm not sure any of us really are. We're young and dumb and think everything revolves around us and our selfish, temperamental needs and flash-bang mood swings, so it's odd to think that the rest of the world went on without us for the past sixty-some-odd days. That beyond the lodge, in the land of internet and phone lines and roads and transit, the people we love have gone about their days; that we weren't integral to any particular aspect of a life; that things have continued and changed without us. Up here, in our state of disconnect, we've changed in a different way. We've sped up and slowed down at the same time—I've gone from buses to boats, from cellphone to crow caw. For the past two months, I haven't worried about school or picking courses for the second year of my master's degree, or writing, or working on my thesis. I've suspended the too-cerebral part of my brain; I've given into the id and listened to my body, not my anxiety. I'm leaner, meaner, ruder. I've learned new swear words and idioms and sayings; I have a new set of knowledge, too, about bear scat and bird calls and boat bottoms. I used to only identify myself as a city girl. Now I know I can exist beyond boundaries marked by telephone poles and highways and subway lines.

I drag my hands through the water, creating that swirl, the pike's surfacing sign of infinity. Around the point, I can hear the dockhands talking to one another, the occasional gem-clear swear word rising above the rest. It seems silly to think that one summer can affect a person so much, that something new is now etched on the innermost parts of me. I wonder if I'm going to be a split woman from now on. That the city life that I always thought was the only life for me will have some doubts pinned to it. I'll remember that I came north with a naive idea of how a summer of hard work could be, and I will remember that I proved myself. That my mettle was more formed and more ferocious than I could have ever known. That I could hold my own with the bullies and the braggarts; that I learned how to make female friends and appreciate all facets of their complicated, gorgeous personalities. From this point on, I'm a woman of two souls. I'll value the rough white-sand beaches as much as a hot, gum-speckled sidewalk, the chitter of the grey jay as much as the laughter of women lined up smoking outside of a Toronto bar, the people I've worked alongside as much as the friends I've known my whole life. I wonder if there will be mornings I wake up in Toronto, years later, and stop dead in my tracks as soon as I open my window because I will smell Kesagami on the air, if there will be moments when I hear a song on a store's stereo system that sounds vaguely like a bird call, and I'll cock my head and wonder for a second. The North has pushed its way into me, onto me, and I'll never be able to shake it.

◦ ◦ ◦

For our final task, Henry decides that the staff has to make new boat rails. With the summer almost done, we feel as if our workload should be lightening. No such luck. It's not just about nailing new pieces of wood in place; to set up the new rails, we're going to have to fill new gabion baskets, large mesh cubes that get loaded up with rocks and are set in place along the shore to prevent erosion. After the gabions are down, the rail can be installed overtop. In order to do both of these things, to get the rails in place exactly where Henry wants them, the entire shoreline is going to have to be moved back about four feet.

When Henry rounds us all up and tells us, I don't quite understand the gravity of what we're going to have to do, but some of the veterans do, and I can see through their dropped jaws and the wideness of their eyes that what's just been asked of us is something more than the usual afternoon chores of staining cabin decks or hauling wood or dropping buoys. There's something more serious about this one.

Four feet. This short distance means digging through four solid feet of compacted, untouched northern soil. This means hauling thousands of pounds of rock—from the shallows, the shore, and the islands—to fill the baskets. This means cutting down tall spruce trees and peeling the trunks, nailing them up in place as new, dangerously slick rails. And all we have are a few rusty shovels, one rogue pickaxe, and seven days in which to complete the task.

It doesn't help that it's so hot it feels as if we're moving through gelatin. The heat is so big and thick that we start every morning in a sweat, being pried out of sleep in a damp panic, emerging from fever dreams so vivid we can't tell if we're awake or still sleeping. It's so hot that we've started wearing our bathing suits under our clothes, so that whenever we have a moment, we can run out into the shallows and sit cross-legged in the water, up to our necks. It's so hot that we snap at one another, our patience wearing thin under the grinding sun and the list of work that stretches in front of us.

It also doesn't help that the final guests at the lodge are officials from the Moose Cree First Nation, people who are technically our bosses, with the transition virtually complete. There are about twenty in their group, which has two ramifications. First, we have to be on our best behaviour because it's like we have twenty managers looking over our shoulders; Henry is even more anal-retentive than ever, making us rewash tables and polish cutlery and refill syrup bottles when we should be focused on winding down for the summer. Second, we can't focus on getting closing-up chores started because we have such a large group in camp—they're flying out on the morning of the last day, leaving us barely any buffer until we, too, have to head home.

"Gonna be a shitshow," Jack mutters when Henry tells us of the plan to have such a big group in camp until the last possible moment. "A real fucking shitshow."

That afternoon, every member of staff on shore—dockhands, housekeepers, guides who aren't out on the lake—lines up along the water's edge. We're dressed in our sloppiest clothes, caps pulled low on our heads. The sun is as fat as I've ever seen it, ripe as a large, hard fruit, birch-white and searing, and I can feel the back of my neck prickling with heat, see silver spots swim across my eyes when I try to turn my head too quickly. There are several rusty shovels and the one wobbly pickaxe strewn on the ground, and someone has spray-painted a red line four feet back from where the shore currently ends: this is our finish line, the place we need to shovel our way to.

There's no ceremony. We pick up the tools and we start. It goes like this: someone uses the shovel, and someone is in charge of the wheelbarrow. The digger fills the barrow; the barrow-driver wheels the dirt over to the side of the shore, dumps it as far away as possible, and comes back for another load. I thank God we're not on the Canadian Shield, because then this inane task would be near impossible. Still, the soil we're gnawing into is difficult: it's heavy and almost clay-like, filled with rocks and roots, and garbage that was left behind by the years of guests and construction before us and compacted back into the earth like awful fossils.

We're a chain gang, driven on by the metronome of the *thunk-ca-chunk* of our shovels hitting the hard dirt, prying a load loose, dumping it into the drum-like belly of the barrow, going back for seconds, thirds, fourths, until it feels like our arms are going to fall off, like our biceps are burning and our heads are hazy-stupid and we're about to fall over, swooning into the dirt.

At some point, I end up next to Jack, who has somehow become my wheelbarrow partner as I clumsily manipulate a shovel. I look around for Tiffany, not wanting to upset the status quo, but she's gone inside to run the dinner service, so I'm stuck with him.

I nod to the pickaxe at his side.

"Can I use that?" Already, I'm kicking myself for feeling the need to ask him for permission.

Jack looks at it. "Oh, Jesus," he says, shaking his head, picking it up as if he's trying to get it out of reach. "No. Absolutely not."

I wrest it from his hands anyway. If I'm going to be working my ass off, I might as well have fun, and the pickaxe looks like it could be pretty entertaining.

I swing, and hit my shin.

Jack howls with laughter. "You idiot."

I've managed to knock myself above my protective work boot. The bruise is going to last for days. I resist putting the pickaxe right through his head.

There must be something desperate in my face, because he softens. "All right, here, look. You have to do it like this." He swings the pickaxe and slices through a ream of soil, using his weight like a lever. He makes it look easy, seamless, as if his arms aren't about to fall off, as if there isn't sweat tracing its way from his hairline down his spine. I scratch at the damp waistband of my pants, fan my shirt away from my body to try to get some air next to my skin. Jack straightens up and wipes the back of his hand across his forehead.

"Give it," I say, pulling the tool to my chest. While I'm not as apt as him, my second try isn't so clumsy, and I knock some dirt onto the ground. He shovels it into our waiting wheelbarrow. I do it again, and feel powerful, feel my brain start to let go and give in to my body and its ability to work. The hiss and chunk of the pickaxe's movement makes a slow song, and my heart starts to fall in line with the tempo.

And that's how it goes. We all become a soft rhythm of swinging, hitting, swinging, the clank of the shovel against the wheelbarrow's sides, the *click-clack* of the barrow's wheels over shoreline pebbles, the occasional muffled swear word, the sporadic yelp of a tired joke. As the day wears on, the sun bears down on the backs of our necks and the tops of our heads. The boats throw long, cool shadows; when we need a break, we squat beneath the hulls. I swirl my baseball cap in the shallows, avoiding the algae and dead-bug bodies, and slap the hat back on my head, feeling the lake water trickle down the back of my neck, joining the trails of sweat. As the sun gets stronger, our vocalizations become fewer, until finally we're working in hot silence, conserving all possible energy for the up-and-down and back-and-forth motions of digging and dumping and digging and dumping. Our break times are spent staring blankly at each other, stunned from the heat and the exhaustion. *Drink water*, Jack and Pea urge, and we take frequent Thermos breaks, curling up in the shade.

Each inch of dirt becomes a ribbon of accomplishment. Each barrow is a medal we wish we could wear on our chests. Really, we don't have to finish the new shoreline. We could, theoretically, tell Henry to shove it. We could tell him that next year's staff can finish what we've started if he wants new boat rails so badly. That it's a stupid task to do in the final few days before we leave, and that there's so much else to get done. But we have pride.

At one point, Connor unearths a flat piece of rock and dusts it off. Without saying anything, he slams it into the ground so it's sitting up like a tombstone. Pea takes a piece of charcoal and writes *R.I.P. Henry* on it. It stays on the shoreline for the rest of the day. If Henry sees it, he doesn't say anything.

•   •   •

After the digging, there are the rocks to contend with. Jack and Pea do some rudimentary calculations and figure out we're going to apparently need about thirty thousand pounds of stones to fill the gabion baskets that now sit in position, empty and with tops open wide like hungry maws.

"Are you fucking kidding me?" Syd hurls a pebble in their direction.

"I didn't choose to do this!"

"What the fuck, man—"

And so goes the unceremonious beginning to the new stage of our labour—hauling. But this is no ordinary rock collection, not like the times all the housekeepers would join hands and walk through the shallows off the main beach, sweeping their legs back and forth to feel for rocks to pry out of the silt and bring back to shore to line the lodge paths. This is not gentle. This is, instead, like every wood and rock haul from the entire summer is compressed into one awful task—with a time limit.

We walk up and down the shore, starting with the smaller rocks that are easy to grab, palm-sized and the perfect heft. When we run out of those—which happens too quickly—we move on to the larger stones. We squat, shoving gloved fingers into silt, prying rocks out of shore mud. We crawl under boats. We crawl under branches. We crawl into the cusp of the forest. We use sticks and shovels and other rocks as tools, anything and every-thing to get the stones out of the ground and into the gabions. When we run out of rocks on shore, we slide off the end of the dock and walk, knee-deep, through the water, wrestling stones out of the mud, getting the hems of our shorts and shirts wet as we dig. When we get a rock loose, we throw it into a wheelbarrow

Kev is holding steady on the dock. As we're doing that, the other guys focus on the boulders that have probably sat undisturbed in the ground for decades, centuries, maybe longer. Jack and Pea build a makeshift pallet out of four old wooden boards, and the guides and dockhands work to roll each big stubborn rock onto the pallet and struggle to carry it to the baskets.

Suddenly, there's a scream, and then a squawk, and then a splash. I whip my head around to look. Kev—and the wheelbarrow—have disappeared off the dock. Alex and Alisa are standing knee deep in the water, mouths open, hands to their faces. There's a moment when I'm frozen with cold fear.

"Oh, what the fuck, Rook!" Jack's voice carries, sharp and cutting.

I stand up from where I've been crouched under the boats, dart up to the concrete part of the shore, and once I get a better vantage point, I can see what's happened. Kevin, who was trying to wheel the barrow up the narrowest part of the dock, the little wooden gangway plank, lost his balance and took a header into the shallows—along with the load of rocks. He's fine, thank God, standing up with both pointer fingers in the air to shrug off his fuck-up, showing off the scrape on his inner thigh, but it's another reminder of how quickly things can turn. We throw ourselves into our tasks without thinking about the ramifications, and so far, we've been lucky that no one has suffered a major injury.

"Better pick up those goddamn rocks," Jack continues, gesturing to the water where the wheelbarrow is partly submerged, its belly red and rusty in the sun, and that's what happens. The housekeepers congregate around Kev, look at his bleeding skin.

We make sure he's actually fine, and then lift the barrow out of the water, put the rocks back in, and keep trucking. As always. As per usual. As we've done the entire summer.

We gather rocks for two days straight. We work until the sun falls like a lure toward the hungry line of the horizon. We work until the backs of our necks are on fire, until the tips of our ears are dangerously sunburned and our hair is matted to our foreheads. Until we stink through the green of our shirts and our palms are blistered and flaking and our muscles screaming from lifting huge chunks of granite. Most important, we work until we finish the goddamn job, all of us staring at the new shoreline lined with new gabion baskets sitting four feet back as we assess what we've done. We stand in a row, dead quiet and breathing strong and fast through our noses, our hands resting on the tops of our shovels and pickax and the lips of our wheelbarrows, our bodies silhouetted against the gloaming sky, and we wonder if this will last until next year or the year after that or even the year after that, if what we've done is even a little bit permanent, or if, as soon as we've left, the land will rise up and swallow our work, rip apart our feeble attempts at changing what has been here for eons.

But for the moment, that doesn't matter. We came and saw and changed. We carved ourselves into the landscape, like writing our names on the ceilings of our cabins—and when new staff come, far in the future, Henry can tell them that we did *that*, that we worked together in a choreographed chain, dipping and bowing, arms raised, arms lowered, that this is what that dance built.

*　*　*

Later that night, we all go swimming for the last time. It's less for pleasure and more for necessity, because when we scythe into the lake, clutching bars of soap, the water behind our bodies is feathered with oily trails. When we bob up from submersion, the border on our skin where the dirt used to be is clear and sharp.

This is a quiet swim. We're so tired we can't find it in ourselves to get our tongues working. Every muscle, every body part wants to be still and silent, and so we sit up to our necks and let the water lap against our collarbones. Minute by minute, the sweat and grease and smoke washes off of our bodies; hot skin becomes temperate, less blistered from the days of sun; sore fingers and palms and arches of feet are cooled, and we stretch underwater and feel the meat of our legs and biceps lengthen and untangle. We let the lake take the bad from us and carry it away toward the horizon.

THE BURN

With only three days left until we leave, the chores have gotten thicker and weirder. Dishes I've never seen before are pulled out of storage and washed and put back into storage and then pulled out and washed again when Sam forgets whether he's cleaned them or not. Dirt we never noticed up until now—in the corners of guest bathrooms, on the handles of lunchboxes, on the rungs of racks used to store the lodge's Thermoses—is pointed out and added to our list of things to scrub and wash and bleach, and scrub and wash and bleach again. Food that has stayed in the freezer all summer is defrosted and mismatched meals are presented to us: pitchers of stale Kool-Aid paired with bowls of iceberg lettuce and mushy bananas; bowls of rib sauce put out alongside macaroni salad and freezies on the side; apples piled high on a plate alongside platters of ground beef and wrapped slices of Kraft Singles cheese. We eat all of it with shrugs—in this final maniacal countdown, we're hungry for everything.

And behind it all, underneath it all, we keep the literal home fires burning. Dump burn goes from a kind of unsafe activity to an incredibly unsafe activity: instead of burning just food waste and bathroom-bin trash, the guys have started to burn old wood, garbage from the lodge attic and basement, cardboard boxes, linens that can't be salvaged. Books, hats, rags, mats, any and all detritus the guys can get their hands on. I don't know if this happens every season, but it seems that anything that can't be stored properly—or even some of the stuff that can be—is chucked into a wheelbarrow and trolleyed to the dump.

While lugging firewood to one of our kindling piles, I run into Jack on the back path. I crinkle my forehead; he's sort of hunched over, and there's something imminently suspicious about him, more so than usual. As I pause, Aidan comes cackling around a corner with a bucket, Connor at his heels. They dig their feet into the dirt when they see me, stopping on a dime, and something in the bucket sloshes.

"What're you doing?" I ask, shifting the wood in my arms.

Jack clicks his tongue. He doesn't castigate me, so I'm both wary and intrigued. What has distracted him so much that he's put aside his irritation with me?

"Wanna see dump burn, Big Rig?"

It's rare for a housekeeper to be invited to see the burn, and I feel a bit as if I've been inducted into some clandestine boys' club. I don't want to leave without having witnessed it. Besides, the return of my nickname makes something inside of me melt.

I look at Jack's strange spraddle-legged gait. "Why are you walking funny?" He reaches behind him and knocks on something that makes a wooden sound. There's something shoved down the back of his pants. "Never mind. I don't want to know."

Beside me, Aidan hits the bucket against his shins as he starts to walk, and I realize it's gasoline that they're carrying. The smell is suddenly strong in the air.

"Just you wait," Jack answers.

*　*　*

It's been a tense few days. The Moose Cree guests have been polite—some of the better tables I've served, interested in making conversation and quick to say please and thank you—but they're a large group, and that means lots of work. They're also here for a work retreat, so they're not always out on the lake. Instead, they spend their mornings in the lodge, going over documents and doing presentations, so we have to do our cleaning around them, which means we have to be quiet and straight-laced, which means that we're practically quivering with pent-up energy that we would normally be able to exorcise. We've had to be well-behaved, serious under Henry's hawk eyes—and that feels wrong. We feel loose and rude, ready to go and also not ready, like all our feelings are rattling around inside our heads and bumping up against our skin with no place to go.

There's something else at play, something about race and power dynamics that no one is talking about. When Alex recognizes one of the former Moose Cree grand chiefs at one of the dinner tables, she exhales a sigh of relief that his wife isn't with him.

"Why? Do you know them?"

"They were up here a few years ago," Alex says, trying to get a stubborn stain off of a coffee carafe. We're standing in the dish-pit, talking in hushed tones. "His wife was . . . hard to serve."

"What do you mean?"

"She kept sending her food back, and being kind of rude to me. Eventually, he pulled me aside when she was in the bathroom and said, 'I'm sorry about her, but she just really doesn't like the white man.'"

I blink at Alex, who is still focusing on the carafe spout. "What?"

"I mean, fair," she says. She's not angry, or offended, only recounting the situation. I can't imagine what I would have done if I had been in her place. What would I have stuttered out as a reply?

"What did you say?"

"I don't remember," she says, picking up a piece of steel wool. "I think I apologized, too."

The whole situation is an ouroboros—we, white employees, spending our summer on land that decidedly does not belong to us and never has, but is now in the process of being purchased by the people who I think should have had rights to it all along. No one is talking about race or privilege or tensions, but they're simmering under the surface. This shows itself when Henry is talking to the group about fish quotas for shore lunch, and one of the Indigenous women says, "Well, it's *my* lake; I can take whatever I want from it," and all of the housekeepers kind of titter to ourselves behind our hands, because Henry has no response for that, and neither do we.

Something is also going on with Gus. He's been making the housekeepers' lives more difficult than usual at dinner. Because he's from Moose Factory, and knows the Moose Cree First Nation group, he's been their guide for the afternoons when they do go fishing. But he's been bringing them back later and later each night. I can't tell if that's because the guests want to stay out for as long as they can, or if it's because he hasn't told them about the cut-off for dinner service, but it's making us all pretty anxious. Guests are told to be back in the dining room by 8 p.m. every night, at the very latest, and, in general, most of our guests this summer have followed this rule. But some of our current guests have been coming in at 8:30, or even nine, which has a domino effect. The later the housekeepers serve, the later we get out of the kitchen. The longer we're in the kitchen, the meaner we get. The later Gus comes in off the lake, the less time he has to help the dock-hands and other guides with some of the bigger chores that need to be done before our final day—one of the biggest of them being taking the boats out to the narrows and storing them on the racks out there for the off-season. So something doesn't feel right. I can't tell if it's because Gus is with people he knows from home, so he's already checked out for the summer, thinking about his real life back in Moose Factory, or if it's because there's something else percolating.

I'm not even sure he *likes* the group he's guiding: the morning they flew into camp, I was making coffee in the kitchen, and Gus sauntered in to grab a handful of muffins.

"You watch out," he said around a mouthful.

"What?"

"These women, in this group—you can't trust them. You watch out, girl. They love to talk about people behind their backs," he said, shoving another muffin into his mouth. He drags out the word *love* like a series of round vowels. "Just keep your nose clean."

So I can't tell where he's at, or what he's thinking, if he's feeling split between two semblances of home. All I know is that it feels as if there's a big storm brewing, something spreading out over the horizon. I can sense it in the air, but I'm hoping it clears before it reaches camp.

•   •   •

"Okay. One thing you need to know about the burn—if you hear popping sounds, duck."

Aidan and Connor are walking around the periphery of the dump, sloshing gasoline onto the garbage.

"What? Why?"

Connor calls from across the pit. "Popping means someone"— and here he looks at Aidan, who is merrily unaware—"didn't go through the garbage, and there're still batteries and bottles in there." He points to the trash.

"What?"

"Missiles, Big Rig." Jack makes an exploding sound with his mouth. *Pew.*

"Duck?"

"Gee fucking whiz, you stupid or what? Just find a tree to hide behind or something."

I look around. "Where are the bears at?"

"Hiding. They're probably watching us from the trees. I bet there are two or three near us right now."

Aidan finishes dispersing the gasoline, and the four of us stand elbow to elbow at the spot where the path meets the dump. Far back enough to prevent our eyebrows from getting singed off, maybe. Definitely not far back enough to dodge an exploding battery.

Jack pulls a bible out of his pants.

"Oh, God," I say.

"Exactly! Dum-ta-dum-ta-dum!"

"Where'd you find that?"

"You don't need to know. Who has matches?" He dips the corner of the book into some of the remaining gas. I take a step back. Beside me, Connor is laughing silently; I can feel his body shaking. Aidan looks like a child, so impressed with Jack and his transgressive choice of kindling. I just stare, trans-fixed, horrified.

Jack lights the bible, and yodels some verses as he pretends to read. He's unapologetic, his eyes wild in the pre-dusk light. There's gasoline everywhere—on our hands, on the book, on the lip of the bucket. We're all incendiary, dangerous. Jack catches my gaze over the book. Here we are, aflame; here we are, ready to throw the match to the gasoline.

This is another stupid, wonderful thing to add to my memo-ries, to catalogue about these past two months, the things we've done together, the things that'll stay with me, vivid in my mind no matter how much time passes. If I get lonely, back in the city, I will be able to open that book, flip through the memories like an album, to pick out whatever I need to remember to make me feel better. On a shore day so rainy my eyelashes collect drops of water like dew, Jack teaching me to do headstands against the lodge sign—my boots are too heavy, and I fall again and again until he eventually has to grab my feet and hoist them up, and I caw triumphantly as he rolls his eyes as Max, the older guide, sits at the picnic table, clapping his hands softly. Wade and Aubrey going out for a canoe ride, to the part of the lake where the sun is the biggest and the water quietest, and the two of them talking to each other, releasing stress through the rhythmic dip and flash of the paddles. Robin taking sweet naps in the boys' cabin because they keep their fire low and glowing all day, male hands much better at stoking the coals than us impetuous girls, and Connor and Aidan and Wade never saying boo or kicking her out, only stepping quietly around her to get in and out of the front door. Kevin offering his bunk to tired housekeepers as a place to catch some sleep during the day, keeping his sheets clean and fresh, and me collapsing onto his mattress, tearfully grateful. Pea and I spending a quiet hour together, sewing our socks and pants in the darkened guide-shack, the silence calming, with no need to fill the gap with small talk. Jack holding a dying cedar waxwing in his gloved hands. Eight girls swimming into the dusk, sliding under the water with eyes closed.

"Big Rig, pay attention."

The fire spreads down the spine of the open book, lipping at Jack's dirty fingers. Connor and Aidan bellow at him to *hurry, hurry,* and he finally throws the bible in a lit arc, yelling "Ye shall *burn*" at the top of his lungs, turning back to face us as orange explodes behind him.

Everything in front of us lights up with a dull thrum. The sound is like a deep exhalation, and I feel it stir the hair around my face. Black smoke curls up to the tops of the pine trees.

Aidan howls to the sky. "Good one!"

"Yeah, good one!"

Dump burn doesn't have to be this wild or dangerous. I'm sure Henry would have something to say about this mess, but since the burn falls solely to the employees, our boss really has nothing to do with it. And so, away from prying eyes, back in the forest, heroes are made when the fires are stoked. This is how dockhands ensure their names are passed on through generations of Kesagami workers.

The garbage starts to burn with a thick stench, and then I hear it—*pop, pop, pop-pop-pop.*

Connor turns to Aidan with a scandalized look. "Aidan!"

"Oopsies," Aidan drawls.

"Goddamn. Shield your eyes."

I do, putting a hand up in front of my face. As the fire burns, Aidan uses a rake to push the edges of the garbage into the hot centre. Dirty embers, overwhelming heat, and the ripe smell of burning trash fill our nostrils. I'm breathing in our hard work, the discarded cleaning rags, paper towels, the old mop heads, the used sponges and tampons, dishrags, and coffee grounds. It brings tears to my eyes for so many reasons.

I look around and try to stare between the thick trees, and then Connor makes a surprised sound and points up. I follow the trajectory of his finger. Above us, the little female bear clings to a slender tree branch, watching us. I can tell she's inquisitive— kind of frightened, kind of curious. I smile. She's probably been chased up the tree by the older male bears and the fear of the fire. I'm not scared. I incline my head at her as we filter off to the main camp. Behind me, the fire claws at the edges of the dirt, trying to extend its reach.

* * *

On our final night in camp, the dockhands and guides and housekeepers congregate in the guideshack. The final full day of work whizzed by, and this last night feels rushed, as if we've been shoved together by unseen hands and ordered to sort out emotions quickly. As I look around at all of the exhausted faces, I realize that we're nowhere near anything like closure. The girls look browbeaten; the boys look tense. There's a disconnect, and sitting in silence, too tired to talk, won't help that.

It doesn't seem real that we're leaving tomorrow. It's come too fast, roared up on us like some predator that was lying in wait. *I'm here*, it hisses. *I'm here*—goading us, scaring us. Didn't we want to go back home, to the places that we love? We did, or we thought we did. But home has changed meaning now—it's more than just bricks and mortar or a familiar bed or stairs that you can walk in the dark and corners and crannies you know like the back of your hand. It's where and how you make it; it's work and it's hard and it doesn't always make sense, where your love lies and how you start to understand *home* and *belonging* and being *part of something*, but it happens whether you want it to or not and all you can do is let yourself be swept up in it.

I wanted our last night at the lodge to be sentimental: a final evening of huddling together in the guideshack, sitting on the

bunks and wearing borrowed sweaters; maybe even some star-
gazing. I wanted all of us to stay up as late as possible. I pictured
us sitting and watching the dark horizon of the lake until the
sun came up. Something to temper my anxiety about separat-
ing from one another after so many days of sheer togetherness.
Something to reassure me that no matter what happens in the
future, I would always have this strange, strong bond. After
this crazy week, our muscles aching and our brains buzzing, we
deserve a star shower, a rest, some shoulder-to-shoulder quiet.

Instead, we're slumped over, tired in the way that stretches
patience tight like a twanging string. We sit without speaking,
without moving, staring into the stove with a dull-eyed accep-
tance. I lean into Aubrey and Alisa, wanting just to close my
eyes and rest, to feel the solid warmth of these other women
and not think about tomorrow.

Then I hear the front door open and some unfamiliar voices.
I crack open an eye to see Gus with two Moose Cree guests. All
of the staff freeze in place. Guests in the guideshack are a rare
occurrence. If we do bring guests to the staff cabins, it's usually
because they're young, or they're exceptionally cool, or they've
been coming here for years and want to thank us for our work
in person for a brief moment. It's far more common for the
staff members to hang out in the guest cabins. It's more neutral
ground. Fewer personal effects; less room for trouble. Having
guests in the guideshack is a recipe for disaster.

Gus has a string of freshly caught walleye in his hand. From
across the room, I see Jack's head snap up. His eyes glow in the
stove light like a predator at dusk. I feel a shudder down my
spine, can't quite figure out why or what's going to happen, but

already the air has started to thicken with something about to be unleashed.

Gus is laughing, and his two guests sit down on the small benches around the cabin stove. The staff move off. The boys look at one another with narrowed eyes as they give up their seats; the girls break formation and go and perch on the bunks, in the rooms and out of sight. I don't know what he's going to do with those fish, but the guys sure do. All of the players move into position slowly and surely, setting up the scene: Pea comes to the doorway of his room, shielding the girls behind him with his broad body; Jack leaves Tiffany on his bunk and stands up, keeping his sharp green eyes on the walleye; Kevin hovers in the background. Around me, the girls chat in that mellifluous female way—trying to defuse the situation by keeping conversation flowing like a stream while pretending that nothing's going on—but everyone can see Pea's rigid posture, the way his shoulder muscles flex slightly under the faded green cotton of his shirt.

If Gus senses that something is amiss, he doesn't give a shit. He flips an old bucket over, lays a plank of wood overtop of it, and starts to fillet.

I don't know much about fillet etiquette, when or where to carve up a walleye. I've only done it in the wild open, on an upturned bucket on a boat on shore, on a shitty paddle at a shore lunch. Throughout the summer, there were a few nights when the boys sneaked fresh-caught fish into camp and fried up a late-night makeshift shore lunch in a tiny cooker behind the guideshack. Those were good nights, defined by the hot flake of walleye meat across our tongues, and the roofs of our mouths getting sweetly burned by beer batter and canola oil. But the fish always came into the cabin filleted or cooked. The dirty work was done outside.

Suddenly there's a blare of voices and expletives, and the girly chatter stops. While the words were strung together in an angry elision, and almost unintelligible, the tone was unmistakable: real rage. It's the kind of tone that makes all conversation around it skid to a stop. I see the physical reactions in each of the housekeepers, the shoulders tensed, the eyes widened, the lips ajar. We all knew this was coming, the impending violence, and now we're trapped and will have to weather it, all of us.

I peek around Pea's body, my chin hooked on his shoulder, my body almost pressed to his. I can feel his pulse abruptly quicken, and the way his back becomes tight against the softness of my skin. In the middle of the main room, Jack is standing in front of Gus. The fillet board and the bucket and the fish have been forgotten, and the two guests are silent and expressionless, standing near the door. Gus's face is unreadable, but Jack is moving his jaw as if he's chewing gum, and they're both very, very angry.

"You shouldn't be filleting inside. That's filthy," Jack says. His voice is pure venom, a snake ready to strike.

"Shut up, Jack," Gus answers, a deep, dark rumble.

All eyes are on the two men, and all noise has stopped. We're frozen in a tableau, hands half-raised and mouths half-open. I'm pinned in place. I can't look to see if the guests are watching this unfold, if they realize the trouble that's been caused. All I can do is keep my sights on the rage that's percolating between the two men in front of me.

"This is a fucking disgrace, Gus. You don't fucking fillet inside a cabin," Jack says, staccato.

"Don't you talk to me that way in front of the guests," Gus counters. "They're your bosses now, you know." It's the wrong thing to say, and he knows it. We all know it, and there's a low sound as a bunch of us exhale.

Jack rotates his head on his neck; I recognize that motion as him being about to verbally lash out. Pea steps forward again, now almost out of the doorway. My heart gallops, trying to tear out of my chest. I flick my eyes over to Kev, in the corner of the room, half in shadow. His eyes are hard, and his hands are balled into fists at his sides. That's when I get genuinely scared— if Pea and Kev, our two beautifully happy young men, are moving into attack formation, it's possible that something terrible is going to happen. Gone are the jolly smiles, the gentle jokes and tough love and kindness, and in their place is hardened young masculinity, brashness in full bloom. Can Pea feel the way my blood is roaring through my body, the way my chest is starting to heave with barely suppressed panic? If he does, he shows no notice. Instead, I watch—feel—as his hands, which were in his pockets, slowly unsheathe themselves, curl at his sides to mirror Kev, two sentinels readying themselves for a battle that may or may not happen, depending on how the men in the eye of the storm handle themselves.

"Oh, Jesus Christ." Jack says the words like he's spitting. My head snaps back to them. "All summer, you've been nothing but *lazy*. You keep bringing guests in so fucking late that the girls can't even serve them properly."

Gus counters so quickly there's no space to even take a

breath. "You know what your problem is, Jack? You're a rat. You rat people out to Henry. People can't even fucking trust you, because you just go running to the boss. Running your mouth."

"Fuck off, Gus." The words are said with such vehemence that, suddenly, it's like we're all pushed back against the walls, held in place by the virulence. Every single good thing we did this summer—every bridge we built between our different factions, every piece of affection we drew out of one another, every touch we branded onto one another's bodies as a way to remember the work we did, the love we forged, the beauty we created—suddenly shatters. It rips like a fault line, leaving some of us on one side of the divide and some on the other. It hurts so much that I can feel it in my meat and bone, this tearing of the bonds, this cracking of the veneer, and I shake with it. I hear a sound like a gasp, a broken sob, and I realize that it came from me.

In the maelstrom, between the two men, some unsaid line has been crossed. Gus steps up to Jack and the tension peaks to a shimmering point. I feel pure fear jag through me. For all we think we know about one another, I realize we really don't know shit. I have no idea about Gus's past, or what he's capable of. His physical presence is suddenly overpowering. He's gone from a trickster to an angry bear, and the unfolding interaction fills the room with flames.

The two of them stand there, face to face, for a long moment. Gus is much bigger than Jack and stands over him by a head and shoulders, but Jack doesn't bend away. They're so angry that it hurts the back of my throat.

Gus speaks.

"In my younger days, Jack, I would've broken your jaw for the way you were speaking to me." His voice is low and strange. I've never heard him talk like this. "Just be thankful I'm an older man now."

To his credit, Jack doesn't flinch. I truly believe he isn't scared. Maybe he thinks he'd be faster than Gus if he had to run. Maybe he's cocky enough that the fear has no space to bloom. Jack doesn't move, doesn't blink. His eyes are fixed on Gus, while all of our eyes are fixed on them. I can feel Pea beside me, ready to spring into action if he has to. I can feel all the girls around me, huddled and confused and wondering how it all went to shit so quickly. I can feel the summer breaking apart.

And then, just like that, Gus moves. He steps away from Jack, never taking his eyes off of him, and leaves the cabin. The guests follow silently.

"Oh, God," Pea murmurs, exhaling. "I knew Jack wouldn't be able to take him by himself, so I was getting ready to step in. Gus could break legs, if he wanted to. I think he broke someone's back, once."

I'm already halfway out of the guideshack, Pea's voice trailing off behind me. I've thrown the door open into the swath of deep night, no hesitation, and I'm gone, I'm gone, I'm running away from this bullshit, this mess. I can hear the other girls behind me, also taking flight, but none of us has a flashlight, so we scatter, skittering down different paths on our different journeys tonight, and I just run, run, run, letting my feet pick the route, flashing by cabin after cabin, glowing windows snuffing out as guests bunk down, and then I'm standing on the staff beach, alone, panting. I crouch down, sitting on my haunches, and put both of my hands, palms down, in the water. It laps around my wrists, cool and familiar and frightening all at once. This is my goodbye. There will be no good night tonight; we've ruined it with our fire. We were all complicit in what just happened—why didn't one of us step in? I'm young and female; it wouldn't have killed me to slide between their two taut bodies to defuse the tension. I could have trickled in, water to the burn, to cool it. I dig my fingers down into the lake silt, pushing past the pebbles. *I'm here*, I think. *I'm here*. I don't dare go any farther or stretch my fingers out. I don't dare look to either side of me, not sure what else I'll see on haunches, watching me. I wonder if tomorrow morning someone will find my footprints, or maybe prints of something else. *Where are you?*

I bring my wet hands out and put them to my face, smelling that brackishness, that smell of fish scales and guts and glory. When I start to cry, I'm not sure if I'm actually crying, or if it's the lake water, or if I'm just dissolving, leaving great pieces of myself on this shoreline, so comforting and threatening at the same time. And then I let loose just one sound—a howl steeped in loneliness and uncertainty; that vocalization to find others of its kind; the scream of *are you there, it's me, it's me, I'm here, I'm here, I'm here*—before I take one deep breath, push myself to my feet, wipe my hands on my pants, and turn from my last look at the great, glorious lake cloaked in nighttime.

*   *   *

The next morning, tensions are high. We stagger into staff breakfast wooden and without appetites. Gus and Connor aren't at the table, and Henry tells us they won't be around to help us pack up camp because they're both heading back to Moose Factory with the Moose Cree officials.

I look over at Jack. He's expressionless. Pea just shakes his head, looks down at his plate. Everyone else chews robotically, tired and crease-faced from a bad night's sleep. Maybe Henry assumes we're all hungover, because he rolls his eyes at us and moves along, but we're worse than that, unfeeling and feeling too much at once. I shove a forkful of eggs into my mouth, swallowing without tasting.

"Gonna be a lot of fucking work without those two," Jack says, throwing his spoon onto his plate with a terrible clatter. Around the table, everyone tries not to make eye contact, staring at the ceiling, their crossed cutlery, the smiling faces in the staff photos.

Later that day, I say my goodbyes to Gus and Connor. We're standing near bags of fishing gear and bad-weather clothing and rods and tackle boxes, and everybody is packing, getting onto planes, moving around us as I stare at them. There's so much to be said—*you jerks, you assholes, I'll miss you, you scare me, you made me laugh so much this summer, I'll miss you.* I can't even open my mouth. *I'll miss you.*

Instead of meaningless sentiment, Gus reaches out and squeezes me tight to his body, so much that I can't breathe. "Take care of yourself," he whispers, and I think he's crying.

WHAT WE LEAVE BEHIND

The last few hours before we fly out of camp are the busiest of my entire life. There's a giant list of chores to be checked off in way too little time to get anything done in any kind of organized way. The housekeepers and guides and dockhands run around in ragged, slipshod teams, throwing shore-lunch pans into lockboxes and scrubbing Thermoses with old toothbrushes and making sure the dump doesn't have any live embers left in it and hammering damp pieces of old plywood over windows. At one point in the afternoon, Pea and I are standing on the roof of the lodge, him holding a sheet of wood over a pane of filthy glass and me clumsily wielding a power drill, and all I can think is *Jesus, let this roof hold, please, Jesus.* There's nothing systematic about this process: it follows in the same vein of the summer—haphazard, half-assed, trimming corners whenever Henry's back is turned. Mattresses are piled sloppily and shoved into corners; taps are slammed closed and stoppers thrown into place in sinks; floors are hastily swiped with a mop; food that hasn't been eaten is hurled into the garbage; our silly little summer lives are shoved into our duffel bags. The rooms are closed up. The cabins are locked. Bedsheets get thrown over all the taxidermied animals in the lodge, and there's a brief moment when I stand in the middle of the main building, and the windows are all boarded up so only a reddish-gold light filters through the decorative stained glass at the very peak of the roof, and the kitchen appliances are unplugged, and the covered animals look on like ghosts, and there's only the sound of the dust held in the air like in a joke snow globe, and it's quiet and I'm trying to say goodbye.

* * *

We stand on the shore and watch as the zippy little Otter plane carrying Henry and Sam and Pete gets smaller and smaller on the horizon. Part of me can't believe that our manager isn't staying around to oversee the last frantic throes, and part of me understands: this is the final test in a summer-long string of tasks in which we've been given too much responsibility with too little reward. This is what we've been building up to.

We linger, staring until the Otter disappears. Jack and Pea have been left in charge, and I turn to them for guidance when Pea's head snaps up from where he's been fiddling with the lock on the dockhands' shore box.

"Oh shit."

"What?" Tiff looks at him.

"The narrows."

"Goddamn," Kevin hisses.

"What?" I'm confused, looking at their panicked faces.

"Gus was supposed to help us store the boats in the narrows," Pea says with a sigh. "But we never got around to it because he kept coming off the lake so late."

"He's the strongest of us," Kev adds.

"What do you mean, store the boats?" I ask.

"The strait, it's sheltered, remember—" Pea starts, sounding worried, and then I gasp, because I do remember what he's talking about and a terrible feeling shivers down my whole body, pooling in my shoes. The narrows: that part of the lake where it's more sheltered, where the boats are kept after everyone leaves the lodge. The thousand-pound boats.

"So we—"

"Yeah," Jack says. "Mother*fucker*."

That's how we find ourselves driving the final few fishing boats out to the narrows, where the two planes chartered to take us back to Cochrane are waiting, the pilots—Woody and Billy—sitting on the pontoons, dragging their fingers in the water and watching. Most of the boats have already been brought here over the past week, and they lie in a line along the shore, cradled by the thick white sand. With the new boats, there are twenty green freight canoes, waiting for us. To do what?

"But where—?"

Jack and Kev and Pea point to a few rickety-looking wooden racks higher up on the shore, camouflaged in that their weathered wood is the same colour as the tree trunks of the forest behind them.

I whip my head around to look at the boys, who are grim-faced. "But those racks are—"

"Yeah."

Those racks are at least fifteen feet up on the shore is what I wanted to say, but the situation is so dire that speaking in fragments is the best I can do. We're down men, and are going to have to rely on the housekeepers—minus Syd and Aubrey, who were hurriedly shoved onto a Beaver an hour ago, to be flown into Cochrane to secure our motel rooms for the night before the train ride tomorrow morning.

We split up into teams of two, line up on either side of each boat, and push, pull, push, pull, push—in painful increments, the fudgy sand hampering and slowing us every step of the way—until we get the boat up on shore, near the racks. Then we have to slowly, carefully, anxiously lift the boat to shoulder height, get it onto the rack, and then—finally, warily, so no one gets their hands caught under a thousand-pound freight canoe coming down like a guillotine—flip it so that it's stored with its bottom to the sky and its innards to the ground.

If I thought digging out the shoreline and filling the gabion baskets was the hardest thing I've ever had to do, I was wrong. I was so wrong. This is ten times harder, slower, more painful. The combination of wet sand and boat bottom is a treacherous one; these boats don't haul like they do when they're being pulled up slippery rails. Instead, each foot is a battle that seems to last an hour—and it doesn't help that instead of an all-male hauling team, we have a motley crew: Jack, Pea, Kev, and Aidan, who are worn down and damp-collared; Robin, strong-armed but tired; Emma, wearing a wrist brace because of what we suspect is a hairline fracture that happened during rock haul; Alex, Tiff, and Alisa, panting; me, hopeless and staring at the endless line of canoes waiting for us to lay our hands on them and send them into the off-season with our sweaty palms.

Without any tackle boxes or seat cushions or accoutrements, the boats are exoskeletons, carcasses of the precious, temperamental behemoths that were such crucial parts of our summer. Even the trails they've left in the sand look as though some great beast has pulled itself out of the water and into the forest and curled up, ready to hibernate and wake again when winter turns to spring. Every time we move on to a new boat, grab it by its gunwales, I imagine a heartbeat, an echo, coming from its hull, see its days out on the water, moments of glory. And then all fanciful images are wiped out of my head as soon as we start to push, and my muscles scream, ragged and sharp and angry, while all parts of me strain and stretch themselves taut as I reckon with this land one last time.

There's also more at stake than just the boats and making sure they're stored properly. We're racing against the clock, against the setting sun, because once it gets dark, we won't be able to fly back and we'll be stuck at an abandoned, locked-up lodge for another night or whenever the pilots can come back to get us. The late-afternoon sun taunts us, but it also signals the passing of the hours, the inexorable evening that will come when we least expect it and open its treacherous fabric onto us. Will we make it? Will we have to stay? Or will we take off just as the sun decides to set, getting into the air by the skin of our teeth?

The process with the boats is so slow and so torturous that Woody comes to shore from his plane and starts helping. Jack and Pea protest, knowing that he's recently had heart problems, but he insists, shouldering his way into the fray, and this simple act of kindness makes me tear up. Billy, a different kind of man, sits in his plane, hollering at us through the window, urging us to work faster so he can get back to Cochrane. We push and pull and flip, and push and pull and flip, trying not to look at the sky or the movement of the sun, keeping our eyes on the sand and the gunwales—

Until we're done. The line of boats has turned into an empty beach, a stretch of pale sand gleaming in the late sun, and behind us, there are only giant snail trails, a reminder of work that will be washed away by the next rainfall. And this is how it ends— one final task that no one will know about come next season, one final burst of work so hard that my muscles will ache for days, the boats shelved and waiting to see us off like a colour guard. We stand opposite them, two rows of beasts lined up, staring each other down, our chests rising and falling in panicky rhythms and our palms aching as we look at our silent rivals.

"Hey! We going or what?" Billy's voice clatters across the water and breaks the moment, and we whip our heads around to check where the sun is in the sky as his plane prop starts and that familiar roar fills the air.

●　●　●

The early-evening departure from the lodge means we take off as the sun is just starting to sink—as Emma, Pea, Kev, and I fling our tired and stinking bodies into the sticky seats of Billy's plane, the sunset traces its fingers around the edges of the windshield; as we lace through the water and taxi and rip up, up, into the thin northern air, the light slants once more onto the muskeg and back up into our waiting faces, and we all become very quiet. The cabin of the plane glows; our bodies glow. Everything around me is bright and the air bracketing us slows my movements and makes my arms and legs tired, heavy like paw prints sunk into wet sand, heavy like Jack on my back, like the memory of last night and the argument that keeps replaying in all of our heads and has been for the past day.

Behind me, the other three have fallen asleep, and they're lying on one another's sweaty shoulders, faces seraphic. They loll with every movement of the plane, their arms crossed over one another's laps and chests, and I marvel at how far we have all come, that the borders between bodies are so blurred that the three of them have woven themselves comfortably into an exquisite knot of sleep. While I stare at them, Billy nudges me and tries to hand me a pen, snickering. He wants me to draw moustaches on their sleeping faces, and normally I would, but I can't bring myself to do it this time; I can't disturb their perfect peace or the sweet, cushioning silence that has filled this space. The three of them are too perfect, too beautiful, too still. No frowns, no swearing mouths. No lingering upset.

In the light of this unfiltered sun, it's easy to forget the harsh words said last night. I can forget the yelling and the way our ranks shattered. I can forget the way my co-workers' bodies looked when held tight and full of rage. I can forget that the summer didn't end the way it should have. I can forget that the future is terrifically uncertain, that I don't think Gus and Jack will ever be friends again, that deep in my bones, I know I won't come back here to work next year. Is this the last time

I'll see this sun, this lush fabric of trees, this huge water, these footsteps of giants?

I struggle for a moment, overcome with a rush of fear—the fear I thought I had conquered, that softness that I tried so hard to leave on the rocks. I want to sleep like my co-workers behind me, but at the same time, I know I have to force myself to keep my eyes open, keep awake, keep absorbing so I can remember this place forever, leave no precious memory behind.

As I start to panic, frightened that I'm abandoning a non-negotiable piece of myself—a core of mettle, sun-dark forearms and chapped palms from boat ropes and wheelbarrow handles, strength drawn from the lake and the trees and my co-workers, pieces I never knew I had within me and am now loath to lose— I think about the bears, trodding their paths for millenniums before me and millenniums to come. Of the bugs, with our blood in their bodies. Of cake left in the forest, of my name written in permanent marker on the ceiling of the back girls cabin, of the books and tampons and pieces of clothing we've left for future staff members. And I think of the people who have deposited dreams here: years of sighs and murmurs that will linger high in the corners of the ceilings of the staff cabins, the many feverish nights spent with hands between legs or fingers in hair, the hours of bodies wearing down mattresses from tossing and turning and no sleep coming because the day was so good or so bad or so much of both things at once, the months of laughter so fierce and so fast that it has to be clapped back with a hand over the mouth just to be able to breathe. I think of the people I have learned to love and could never forget, not ever.

And I think about the northern pike, those brindled, beautiful beasts prowling beneath the water's surface. These fish have seen people come and go; they've seen campfires burned out, settlements and villages and towns created and abandoned. They've spent brutal winters under ice, biding their time; they've spent summers listening to the human squeals that reverberate through the lake's surface. They've been caught, thrown back, caught, thrown back; maybe they've learned from their time on the hook, maybe they haven't. But every year, as the seasons change from too-hot northern summer to too-cold northern winter, and then back again, the fish remain—patient, persistent, surviving no matter what is thrown at them.

And somehow, as our tiny plane flies into the sun and back to what I used to think was civilization, that makes all the difference.

ACKNOWLEDGEMENTS

Thank you:

To my agent, Stephanie Sinclair, who is a buttress and also a force to be reckoned with, who gave me hope and purpose when I was lost, and who made this wild dream a reality.

To my editors, Jenny Bradshaw and Kelly Joseph, for blessing me with nuanced, insightful edits, for always being at the ready when I had frantic questions, and for making me laugh even in the thick of rewrites.

To Jared Bland, for believing me, and being a light in a dark time. And also for cat pictures.

To Carly Watters, Emily Davidson, Devon Murphy, and andrea bennett, talented and patient friends who read early drafts and provided key comments; to my brilliant cabal of MFA writers, many of whom saw bits of this book before it was a book; and to Shannon Busta and Kim Magi, two irreplaceable women who keep me going no matter what.

To the Moose Cree, for hosting us on your land and allowing us to experience the summer that we did.

To the housekeepers, dockhands, and fishing guides: without you, I would have never learned how to use chewing gum as a lure, how to make buoys out of bleach jugs, how to clean shit off of a wall, how to love so ferociously, how to laugh so hard.

And most of all, to my family and especially my parents, Walter and Janet. Everything I've accomplished is because of you and your fierce, sweeping love and support. There are no words to properly appreciate everything you've done for me. I love you.

Essays from this collection have appeared in *Maisonneuve*, *The Malahat Review*, Hazlitt, *Prairie Fire*, and *LOST* magazine. The Ontario Arts Council provided a grant, without which this book would not have come into being.